National Curriculum

Key Stage 2
Age 10–11

PRACTICE PAPERS

Key Stage 2 National Tests
SCIENCE

For the 2000 tests

Letts

The test questions, answers and 'Notes to Parents' contained in this publication are based upon the official test materials provided to schools, but do not reproduce those tests exactly. The official tests are supported by administrative and other guidance for teachers to use in setting the tests, marking them, and interpreting their results. The results your child achieves in taking the tests in this book may not be the same as he or she achieves in the official tests.

First published 1995
Revised 1995, 1997 (twice), 1998,
Reprinted 1996, 1998

Second edition 1999

Letts Educational
Aldine House
Aldine Place
London
W12 8AW

Telephone: 0181 740 2266

Text: © Bob McDuell and Graham Booth 1999
Design and illustrations: © BPP (Letts Educational) Ltd 1999

Series editor: Bob McDuell

Prepared by *specialist* publishing services, Milton Keynes

All our Rights Reserved. No part of this publication may be reproduced, stored in a retrieval system, or transmitted, in any form or by any means electronic, mechanical, photocopying, recording or otherwise, without the prior permission of Letts Educational.

British Library Cataloguing in Publication Data
A CIP record for this book is available from the British Library

ISBN 1 85758 970 X

Printed in Italy by Rotolito Lombarda, Milan

Letts Educational is the trading name of BPP (Letts Educational) Ltd

Contents

What you need to know about the National Tests	ii
Preparing and practising for the Science Test	iv
What your child needs to know	vi
Key information: Life processes and living things	vi
Key information: Materials and their properties	viii
Key information: Physical processes	x
Instructions	xii
Test A (Levels 3–5)	1
Test B (Levels 3–5)	22
Level 6 Questions	44
Answers	49
Determining your child's level	65
Marking Grid	66

What you need to know about the National Tests

KEY STAGE 2 NATIONAL TESTS: HOW THEY WORK

Pupils between the ages of 7 and 11 (Years 3–6) cover Key Stage 2 of the National Curriculum. In May of their final year of Key Stage 2 (Year 6), all pupils take written National Tests (commonly known as SATs) in English, Mathematics and Science. The tests are carried out in school, under the supervision of teachers, but are marked by examiners outside the school.

The tests help to show what children have learned in these key subjects. They also help parents and teachers to know whether children are reaching the standards set out in the National Curriculum.

Each child will probably spend around five hours in total sitting the tests during one week in May. Most children will do two papers in Science and three papers in Mathematics and English.

The school sends the papers away to external examiners for marking. The school will then report the results of the tests to you by the end of July, along with the results of assessments made by teachers in the classroom, based on your child's work throughout Key Stage 2. You will also receive a summary of the results for all pupils at the school, and for pupils nationally. This will help you to compare the performance of your child with that of other children of the same age. The report from your child's school will explain to you what the results show about your child's progress, strengths, particular achievements and targets for development. It may also explain how to follow up the results with your child's teachers.

In addition, the publication of primary school performance (or 'league') tables will show how your child's school has performed in the teacher assessments and tests, compared to other schools locally and nationally.

UNDERSTANDING YOUR CHILD'S LEVEL OF ACHIEVEMENT

The National Curriculum divides standards for performance in each subject into a number of levels, from one to eight. On average, children are expected to advance one level for every two years they are at school. By Year 6 (the end of Key Stage 2), your child should be at Level 4. The table on page *iii* shows how your child is expected to progress through the levels at ages 7, 11 and 14 (the ends of Key Stages 1, 2 and 3 respectively).

Most children will take the two papers for Levels 3–5 in Science. The two papers will contain the same number of marks. Each paper will be 35 minutes long. Extension papers with Level 6 questions are available for exceptionally able pupils. However, answering questions on the extension paper will require some knowledge of the content of Key Stage 3 Science.

What you need to know about the National Tests

- ☐ Exceptional performance
- ■ Exceeded targets for age group
- ☐ Achieved targets for age group
- ▪ Working towards targets for age group

How your child should progress

This book concentrates on Levels 3–5, giving plenty of practice to help your child achieve the best level possible. There are also some Level 6 questions for very able pupils. Do not worry if your child cannot do these questions; remember that Level 4 is the target level for children at the end of Key Stage 2. The bar chart below shows you what percentage of pupils nationally reached each of the levels in the 1998 tests for Science.

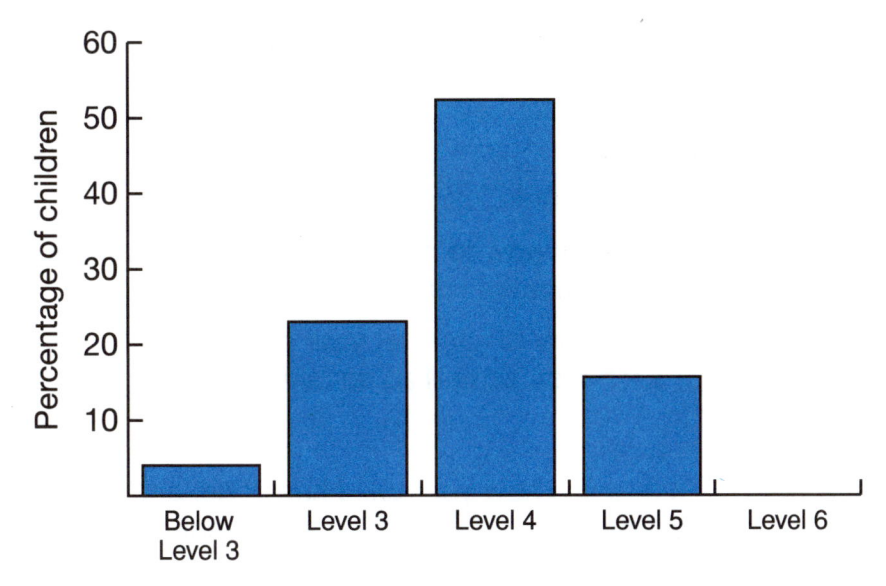

Levels achieved in Science, 1998

Preparing and practising for the Science Test

SCIENCE AT KEY STAGE 2
The questions in this book will test your child on the Key Stage 2 curriculum for Science. For assessment purposes, the National Curriculum divides Science into four sections, called Attainment Targets (ATs). The first AT, Scientific Investigation, is assessed mainly by the teacher in the classroom. The other three ATs are:

- **AT2** Life Processes and Living Things (which is largely Biology)
- **AT3** Materials and their Properties (which is largely Chemistry)
- **AT4** Physical Processes (which is largely Physics).

The National Curriculum describes levels of performance for each of the four Science ATs. These AT levels are taken together to give an overall level for Science. The test papers have questions covering ATs 2–4. National Test questions are designed to assess your child's ability in four areas:

- Knowledge and understanding
- Handling information
- Interpretation and evaluation
- Problem solving.

The questions in this book cover all of these skills.

USING THIS BOOK TO HELP YOUR CHILD PREPARE
This book contains five basic features:

Summary notes	Key information for each Attainment Target, a guide to levels in each of the ATs, sample questions and some quick tests.
Questions	Two test papers for Levels 3–5, and some sample questions for Level 6.
Answers	Showing acceptable responses and marks.
Notes to Parent	Giving advice on how to help your child avoid common mistakes and improve his or her score.
Level Charts	Showing you how to interpret your child's marks to arrive at a level for each test, as well as an overall level.

SETTING TESTS A AND B AT HOME
Try setting Test A first. Mark it to see how your child has done, and work through the answers and advice together. Then set Test B on a different day. Let your child carry out the tests in a place where he or she is comfortable. Your child will need a pencil, a rubber and a ruler. In your own words, describe to your child how to work through the test. Make sure to work through the instructions on page *xii* together.

Note the starting time in the box at the top of each test. During the test, if your child cannot read a word you may read it out. If there is a word that he or she does not understand, you can explain what the word means, providing it is not a

Preparing and practising for the Science Test

scientific word. For example, you can explain what is meant by the word 'label', but not 'force' or 'evaporate'.

After 45 minutes, ask your child to stop writing. If he or she has not finished, but wishes to continue working on the test, draw a line to show how much has been completed within the test time. Then let your child work to the end of the test.

LEVEL 6 QUESTIONS
These are designed for exceptionally able children. Like the actual extension test, these questions are at Level 6 and require knowledge from both the Key Stage 2 and Key Stage 3 Programmes of Study. This means that most 11-year-olds will not yet have covered all the Science topics tested here. Your child should attempt these questions only if the results of Tests A and B suggest that he or she is working at Level 5 or higher. They are included to give an idea of the requirements at Level 6. If your child is not ready to attempt them, you may decide to make use of the material by working through the questions together.

MARKING THE QUESTIONS
When your child has completed a test, turn to the Answers section at the back of the book. Work through the answers with your child, using the Notes to Parents to help give advice, correct mistakes and explain problems. If your child required extra time to complete a test, go through all the questions with him or her, but do not include the marks for the 'extra' questions in the total scores.

Using the recommended answers, award your child the appropriate mark or marks for each question. In the margin of each test page, there are small boxes divided in half. The marks available for each question are at the bottom; write your child's score in the top half of the box.

Enter the total number of marks for each question on the Marking Grid on page 62. Then add them up to find the total for the test. Look at the charts on page 61 to determine your child's level for each test, as well as an overall level.

FINALLY, AS THE TESTS DRAW NEAR
In the days before the tests, make sure your child is as relaxed and confident as possible. You can help by:

- ensuring your child knows what test papers he or she will be doing;
- working through practice questions, and discussing which answers are right and why.

Although the National Tests are important, your child's achievement throughout the school year is equally important. Encourage your child to do his or her best without putting him or her under too much pressure. Many children look forward to tests, but it is natural that some may be nervous. Look out for signs of anxiety, such as changes in eating or sleeping habits, and reassure your child if he or she is worried about these tests.

What your child needs to know

LIFE PROCESSES AND LIVING THINGS (AT2)

Growth, nutrition and reproduction are some of the life processes that are common to all living things, both plants and animals. In addition to these, animals such as humans can move around.

Movement and growth both need a supply of food; to stay healthy the body should receive a diet that is both adequate and varied.

Teeth are important in the digestive process. The incisors are the sharp teeth at the front of the mouth that cut food. The food is ground into small pieces by the molars at the back of the mouth. Between the incisors and the molars are the canines; these are used for ripping and tearing meat or shredding fibrous plant material.

Digested food and oxygen circulate the body in the blood, which is pumped round by the heart. In the circulatory system, blood is pumped through the arteries at high pressure and returns in the veins at low pressure. The pulse rate is the rate at which the heart beats; this increases when more glucose and oxygen are needed due to exercise, and slows down when the body is resting.

The skeleton is the system of bones that supports the body. Individual bones are moved by the action of muscles. While some drugs can be beneficial in treating illness, others such as tobacco and alcohol can have harmful effects on the body.

Animals and plants both have life cycles. In both cases life starts with fertilisation, the fusing of the male and female sex cells to form a new individual. This is followed by the growth of the embryo in humans and seed development in plants. After a human is born, it passes through the stages of childhood and adolescence into adulthood when it has the ability to become a parent. A plant starts life when the seed germinates; after growth it develops sex organs in the flower. Transfer of pollen from the male organ to the female organ may result in fertilisation of an egg in the ovary. The fertilised eggs then develop into seeds.

The growth of a plant depends on environmental factors such as the availability of light, water, a suitable temperature and essential nutrients. The root of a plant has two important jobs; it fixes the plant in the ground and it takes in water and nutrients from the soil. These are transported through the stem to other parts of the plant.

Different habitats can support different plants and animals, depending on the environmental conditions and the food supply. These plants and animals can be identified using keys. The plants and animals in a habitat depend on each other for food. This can be shown by a food chain. Almost all food chains start with a green plant, as green plants make their own food in the leaves using energy from the Sun. Micro-organisms also exist in a habitat. They are essential for decomposing dead material and returning the nutrients to the ground. Some of these micro-organisms are harmful to humans and other animals as they cause disease.

What your child needs to know

Requirements at each level

Level 1 Name the parts of the human body and a plant.
Identify common animals such as fly, goldfish or robin.

Level 2 Describe the conditions needed for plants and animals to survive.
Group plants and animals using simple features.
Know that different plants and animals live in different habitats.

Level 3 Describe differences between living and non-living things.
Explain how changes in living things might occur and recognise how an animal is adapted to its environment.

Level 4 Identify the major organs and organ systems of the human body and a plant. Use keys to identify and group living things.
Use a food chain to describe a feeding relationship.

Level 5 Describe the functions of the organs of the human body and a plant.
Compare the life cycles of an animal and a plant.
Explain why different organisms are found in different habitats and why living things need to be classified.

Quick questions

1. Making new living things is called ....
2. The teeth at the front of the mouth are the ....
3. The heart pumps blood through the ....
4. Humans can stand upright because they have a ....
5. Which part of a plant keeps it fixed in the ground?
   ....
6. Which part of a plant transports water from the root to the leaf?
   ....
7. What do most food chains start with?
   ....
8. Which body organ filters the blood?
   ....
9. What **two** important substances does the blood carry around the body?
   .... and ....
10. In which part of a plant is food made?
    ....

What your child needs to know

MATERIALS AND THEIR PROPERTIES (AT3)

Materials have different properties. These properties include hardness, strength, flexibility and magnetic properties. We choose a specific material for a particular use because of its suitable properties. For example, copper is used for electric wiring because it is flexible and conducts electricity well. It is also easily drawn into a wire.

All substances can exist in three states of matter – solid, liquid and gas, depending upon the conditions. Solids have a fixed shape and volume. Liquids also have a fixed volume and take up the shape of the bottom of the container. Gases fill the whole container. They take up the shape and volume of the container. Liquids, powders and some gases can be poured.

When salt is added to water the salt dissolves. The salt can be recovered by evaporation. This is a reversible change. Other reversible changes are melting, boiling, condensing and freezing. When bread dough is heated in the oven the dough hardens and turns into bread. This change cannot be reversed. Changes involving burning cannot be reversed.

Salt dissolves in water, but sand does not. Filtering can separate a mixture of salt solution and sand.

There is a limit to how much solid can be dissolved in a given amount of water. A solution containing this maximum amount of solid, at a particular temperature, is called a saturated solution. The amount of different solids dissolving in the same volume of water varies greatly.

What your child needs to know

Requirements at each level

Level 1 Observe simple properties of materials.

Level 2 Identify a range of materials and describe similarities and differences between materials.
Sort materials into groups and describe why he or she has grouped them in this way.
Describe how materials are changed by heating and cooling, and by bending and stretching.

Level 3 Sort materials into groups according to properties in a variety of ways.
Explain why some materials are particularly suitable for a particular use.
Know that some changes can be reversed and others cannot.

Level 4 Classify materials as solids, liquids and gases.
Use scientific terms such as evaporation and condensation correctly.
Know that filtration can be used to separate simple mixtures.
Make predictions about whether reactions are reversible or not.

Level 5 Distinguish metals from other solids by recognising metallic properties. Recognise evaporation and condensation taking place in unusual contexts. Know how mixtures such as salt and water and sand and water can be separated. Suggest methods of separating mixtures.

Quick questions

In each of the following lists one material is the odd one out. Which is the odd one out in each list and what property makes it odd?

1 copper   gold   iron   wood
2 cooking oil   ice   petrol   water
3 granite   marble   steel   wood
4 instant coffee   salt   sand   sugar
5 candle wax   petrol   water   wood

Choose words from this list to describe the changes below

burn   condense   dissolve   evaporate   freeze   melt

6 Ice becomes water.   ....
7 Steam becomes water.   ....
8 Oil catches fire.   ....
9 Candle wax becomes liquid.   ....
10 Which of the changes 6–9 are reversible and which non-reversible?   ....

What your child needs to know

PHYSICAL PROCESSES (AT4)

Metals allow electricity to pass through them; they are called conductors. For a bulb to light, there needs to be a complete circuit of conducting material between the positive and negative battery terminals. A switch works by breaking the circuit. In a series circuit there is only one path for the current. A parallel circuit has two or more paths.

How brightly a bulb shines depends on the current. Adding more batteries or increasing the voltage increases the current in a circuit. Adding more bulbs in a series circuit decreases the current and makes the bulbs dimmer.

Forces are pushes and pulls that can be shown as arrows on diagrams. Magnets attract (pull) things made out of magnetic materials such as iron and steel. They can attract or repel (push) other magnets.

The Earth pulls all objects towards it with a force that is called the object's weight; it acts towards the centre of the Earth.

Resistive forces are pushes that act in the opposite direction to movement. All cyclists have felt the effects of air resistance. Friction opposes slipping and sliding; it stops the wheels from slipping on the road and is also used by the brakes to slow the wheels down. To make a bike speed up or slow down the forces need to be unbalanced, so that the force acting in one direction is bigger than the force in the opposite direction.

Pulling on a spring or an elastic band causes it to pull back. Pushing down on the springs in a bed or a chair cause them to push back up so that the upward and downward forces acting on you are balanced and you can lie or sit still.

Stars, lighted lamps and pictures on television screens, for example, can be seen because they give out light, which is detected by the eyes. Other objects are seen by the light that they reflect. When light meets a mirror it is reflected at the same angle as it hits it, but most surfaces scatter light; they reflect it in all directions.

Sounds are caused when an object vibrates. They travel as vibrations of the particles that make up materials and are detected by the ears. The pitch of a sound depends on the number of vibrations per second, and the loudness depends on the size of the vibrations.

The planets in the Solar System orbit (go round) the Sun. Moons orbit the planets. A planetary year is the time it takes for that planet to go once round the Sun. The Earth also turns on its axis, once each day. This causes day and night and makes the Sun appear to move across the sky, from East to West. The Moon's orbit of the Earth takes about 28 days.

What your child needs to know

Requirements at each level

Level 1 Describe changes caused by switching on a bulb and pushing or pulling objects.
Recognise the source of sound or light.

Level 2 Compare the brightness of bulbs and the loudness and pitch of sounds.
Compare speeds and directions of movement.

Level 3 Explain why a bulb does not light or why a sound can only be heard faintly.
Explain how to change the speed or direction of movement of an object.

Level 4 Explain the effect of a switch in a circuit and the formation of shadows.
Describe the effects of magnetic and gravitational forces and how the position of the Sun changes in the sky during a day.

Level 5 Explain how to change the current in a circuit and how to alter the pitch and loudness of a sound.
Recognise when the forces on an object are balanced or unbalanced and describe how objects are seen.
Use a model of the Solar System to explain the length of a day and a year.

Quick questions

Draw the circuit symbols for:

1 a cell   2 a lamp   3 a switch

Which of these forces is a push and which is a pull?

4 Your weight. ....

5 The force between the North-seeking poles of two magnets. ....

In a radio, a loudspeaker makes the sound.

6 How does the loudspeaker cone produce a sound?

....

7 How is it made to produce a louder sound?

....

How long does it take for:

8 The Earth to make one orbit of the Sun? ....

9 The Earth to turn once on its own axis? ....

10 The Moon to make one orbit of the Earth? ....

Instructions

Tests A and B should each take about 45 minutes.

Read all the words carefully. Look at any diagrams or pictures which should help you.

The questions for you to answer are in blue boxes.

For example:

> Give the names of the parts of a flower shown in the picture.

Look for the ✏️ to show you where to write your answer.

Remember to explain your answers if you are asked to do so.

After finishing a page, turn over to a new page without waiting to be told.

If a question is too hard, you should move on to the next question.

Test A

TEST A
LEVELS 3–5

MARKS

Start ☐ Finish ☐

1 The picture shows part of a wood.

a | Tick **two** boxes to show **two** things that both the bird and the tree can do.

fly ☐   grow ☐

lay eggs ☐   produce seeds ☐

reproduce ☐

2
Q1a
Level 3

b | Tick **one** box to show **one** thing that the bird and the swing can both do.

grow ☐   move ☐

reproduce ☐

1
Q1b
Level 3

c | Tick **two** boxes to show **two** reasons why few plants grow under the tree.

it is too dark ☐   it is too dry ☐

it is too light ☐ it is too wet ☐

2
Q1c
Level 3

1

Letts

2 Here is a picture of a seal.

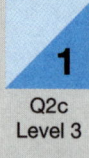

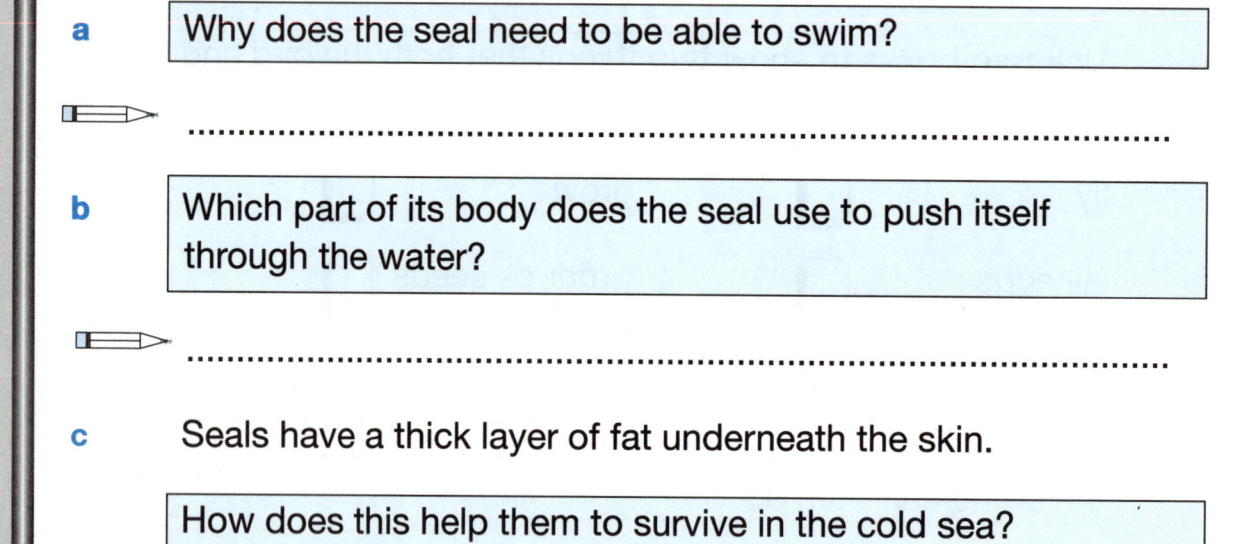

a Why does the seal need to be able to swim?

....

b Which part of its body does the seal use to push itself through the water?

....

c Seals have a thick layer of fat underneath the skin.

How does this help them to survive in the cold sea?

....

Test A

3   Adam planted three lots of cress seeds.
    This is what they looked like after two weeks.

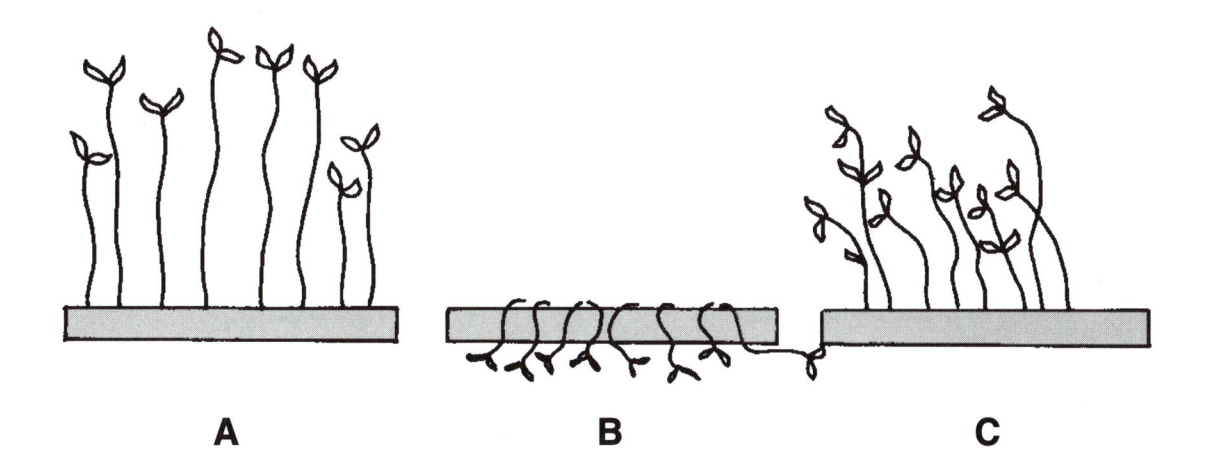

               A   B   C

a   Which plants did he forget to water?

    ☐

b   Which plants did he leave on a windowsill?

    ☐

4 Here is a key. It can be used to identify four small animals.

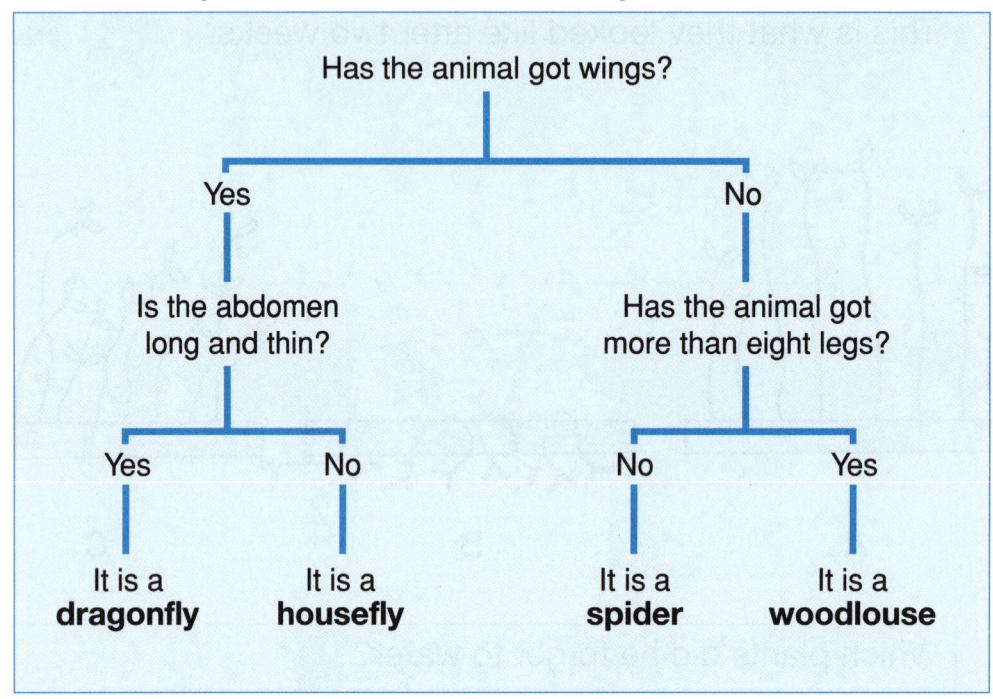

```
                Has the animal got wings?
               /                          \
            Yes                            No
             |                              |
    Is the abdomen              Has the animal got
    long and thin?              more than eight legs?
      /         \                   /            \
    Yes         No                 No             Yes
     |           |                  |              |
   It is a    It is a            It is a        It is a
  dragonfly  housefly            spider        woodlouse
```

a Write down **two** things you could use to help identify a dragonfly.

1 ....

2 ....

b Write down **two** things you could use to help identify a woodlouse.

1 ....

2 ....

c Rebecca finds an animal with eight legs and no wings. What in the key is it?

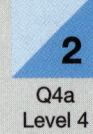

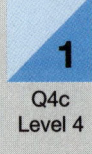

....

Test A

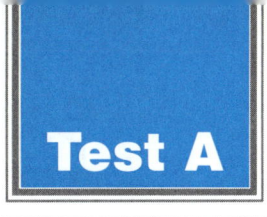

d Rebecca reads that woodlice prefer to live in dark places rather than light places.

What could she do to find out whether this is true?

....

....

....

....

e She goes outside and finds woodlice underneath a stone, near a pond, and in a piece of rotting wood.

What else do woodlice like as well as darkness?

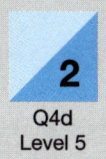

....

TEST A
LEVELS 3–5

MARKS

Test A

5 This question is about the parts of a flower and the job each part does.

a Write a label in each box using words from the list.

ovary   petal   sepal   stamen   stigma

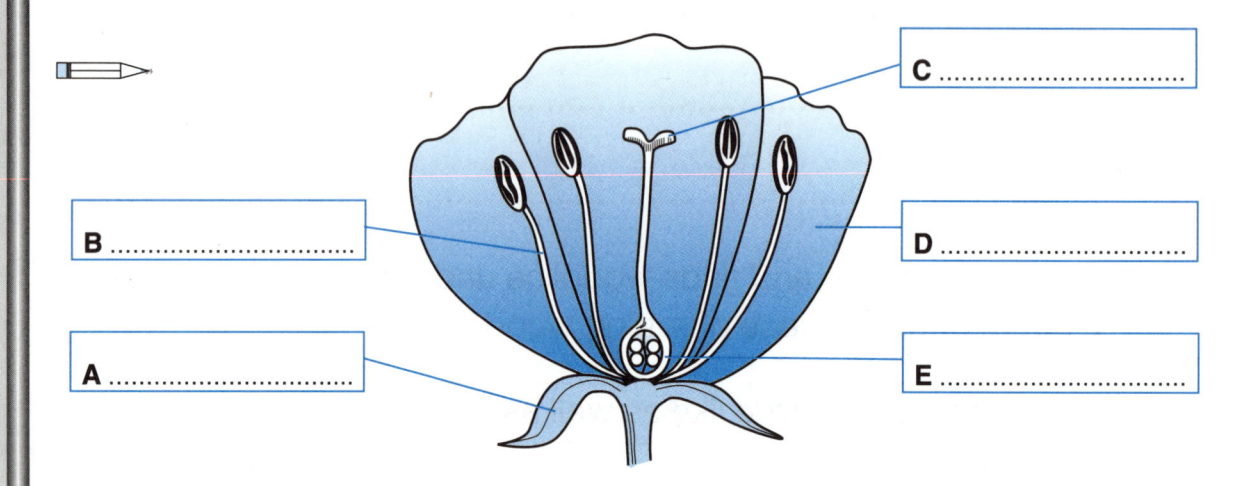

C ....

B ....

D ....

A ....

E ....

4
Q5a
Level 4

b The table shows the jobs of the different parts of a flower.

Write the letter of the correct part next to each job.

Job/part of flower	Letter of part
attracts insects to the plant	
male part of the flower	
where egg cells are made	
sticky part that receives pollen grains	
protects the flower when in bud	

4
Q5b
Level 5

6

6 Sam is fitted with a device that records her pulse rate. The chart shows her pulse rate at playtime.

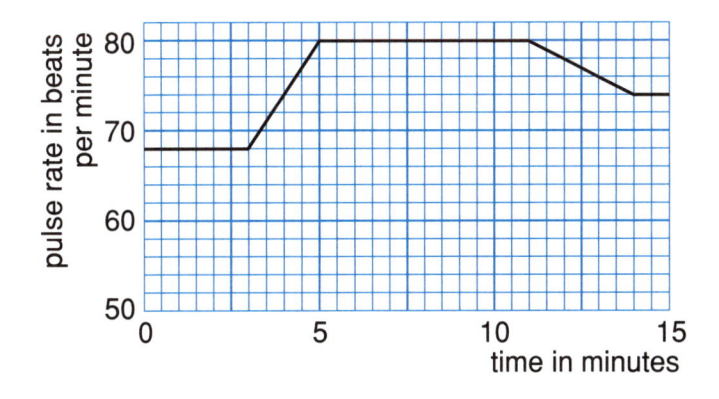

a What was Sam's pulse rate after five minutes?

....

b After three minutes Sam started to run around. How can you tell this from the graph?

....

c Why did Sam's pulse rate change when she started to run around?

....

d When did Sam's pulse rate start to go down again?

....

TEST A
LEVELS 3–5

MARKS

Test A

7   Here are some materials that we use.

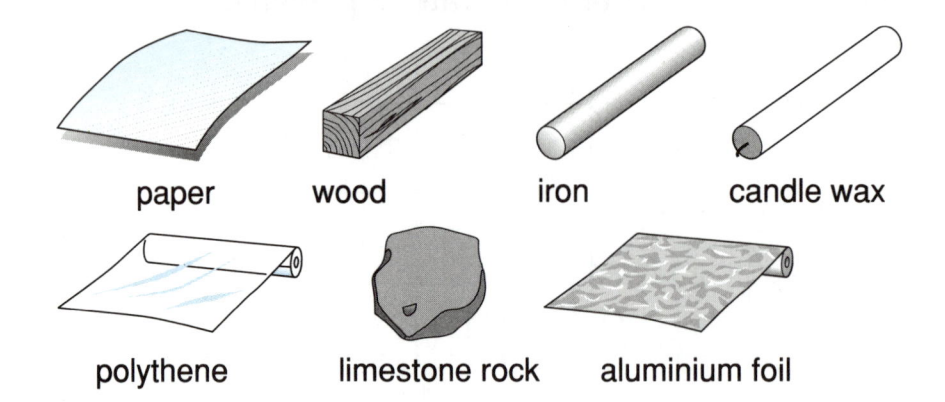

paper   wood   iron   candle wax

polythene   limestone rock   aluminium foil

a   Finish the table that shows the properties of these materials.

material	easy to bend	attracted to a magnet	see-through	soaks up water
paper	✓	✗	✗	✓
polythene	✓	✗	✓	✗
wood				
limestone				
aluminium foil				
candle wax				
iron				

5
Q7a
Level 3

b   Write down **two** reasons why polythene is better than paper for packaging food. Use the table to help you.

....

....

2
Q7b
Level 3

c   Which **two** materials in the table are metals?

....

and ....

2
Q7c
Level 3

8

8   Coffee can be made by pouring hot water onto crushed coffee beans. The diagram shows a machine for making coffee.

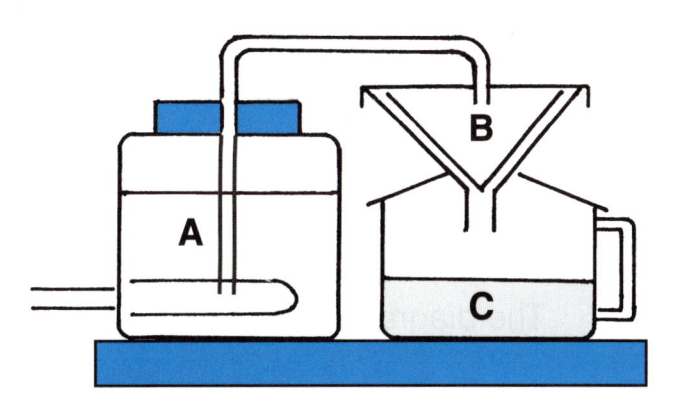

a   In which part of the machine:

   i   is the water heated? ☐

   ii is the coffee solution collected? ☐

   iii does the coffee dissolve in the hot water? ☐

b   In part B the coffee solution is separated from the crushed beans.

   Name the process that is used.

   ....

c   Instant coffee is made by spraying coffee solution onto heated rollers.
   Solid coffee granules are left on the rollers.

   i   Put a ring around the change that takes place on the rollers.

   condensation   distillation   evaporation   melting

   ii Is the change that takes place on the rollers reversible or not reversible? Explain your answer.

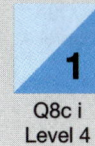

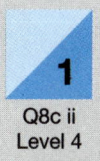

   ....

   ....

9 Rebecca and William want to find out which is the better heat insulator: fur or foam.

They pour boiling water into two beakers. One beaker has fur wrapped round it. The other one has foam wrapped round it. The temperature of the water is measured each minute. The diagram shows what they use.

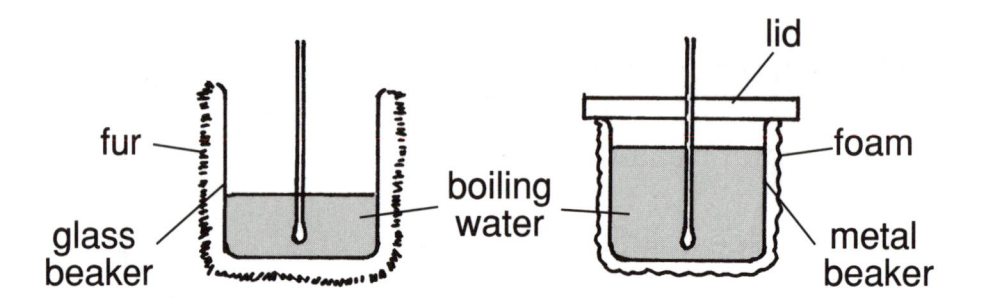

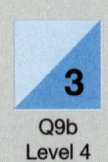

a What do they use to measure the temperature of the water?

....

b Write down **three** reasons why their test is not fair.

1 ....

2 ....

3 ....

They repeat the experiment making sure this time that the experiment is fair.
They draw a graph of the temperature of the water in the fur-lined beaker. The graph they draw is on the next page.

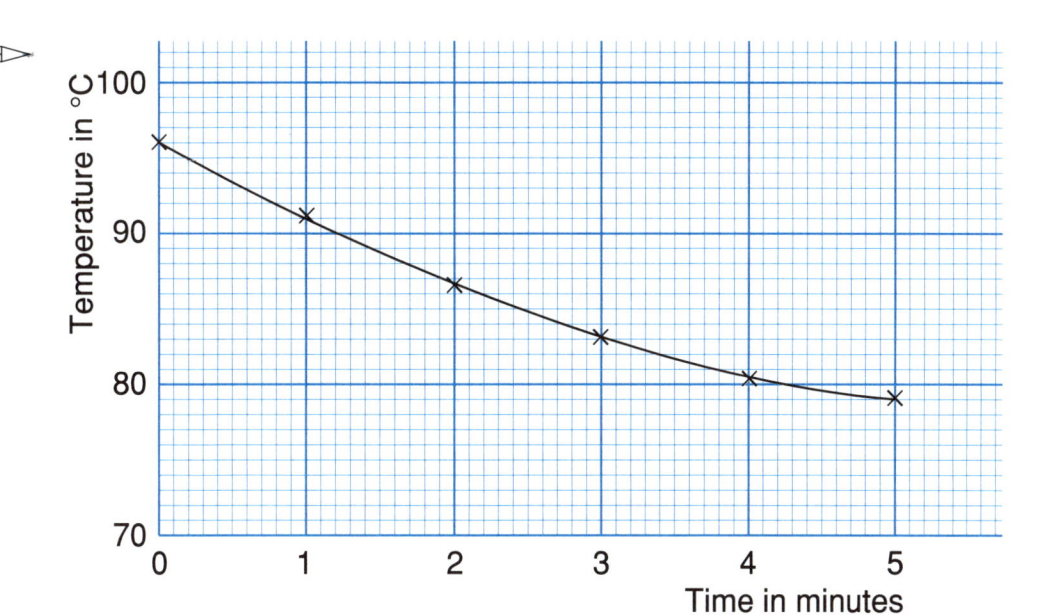

c What is the temperature of the water in the beaker after 3 minutes?

.... °C

Here are their results using the beaker wrapped in foam.

Time in minutes	0	1	2	3	4	5
Temperature in °C	96	90	84	78	74	70

d On the same grid plot their results for the beaker wrapped in foam. Draw the best curve.

e How do they know that fur is a better insulator than foam?

....

....

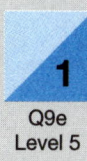

TEST A
LEVELS 3–5

MARKS

Test A

10 The drawing shows part of the water cycle.

The table shows the five stages in the water cycle.
Finish the table by writing in numbers to show the correct order. Number 1 has been written in for you.

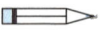

water condenses to form clouds	
water runs into the sea	
water falls as rain	
water evaporates from the sea	1
water vapour rises in the air	

3
Q10
Level 5

11 Some ice cubes are placed in a glass of water.

a What happens to the temperature of the water after the ice cubes are placed in the glass?

....

1
Q11a
Level 4

b Explain why the outside of the glass becomes misty.

....

....

2
Q11b
Level 5

12

12   Ahmed and Hayley are playing with a bat and ball.

Ahmed throws the ball and Hayley hits it back.

a   Tick **two** things that change when Hayley hits the ball.

   the colour of the ball ☐

   the direction of the ball ☐

   the shape of the ball ☐

   the weight of the ball ☐

b   Tick **two** things that change as the ball travels through the air.

   the colour of the ball ☐

   the height of the ball ☐

   the speed of the ball ☐

   the weight of the ball ☐

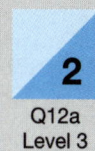

13 Chris makes this circuit.

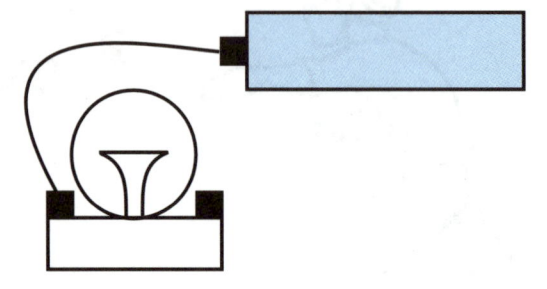

a Why does the lamp not light?

....

b What should he do to make the lamp light?
Draw it on the diagram.

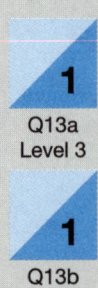

14 On sports day, four runners line up to start a race.
They set off when they hear the noise from the starter.

Mary Rose Gutja Sarong

a   Who hears the loudest noise?

    ....

b   Explain why she hears the loudest noise.

    ....

c   The runners start as soon as they hear the noise.

    Who is last to set off?

    ....

d   Explain why she is last to set off.

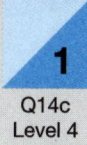

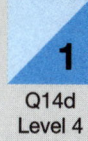

    ....

15 A driver sets out early in the morning on a long journey.
The Sun is low in the sky.

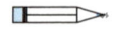

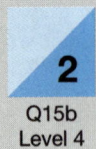

a | The driver can see a puddle on the road.
Draw a line on the diagram to show how the driver can see the puddle. Label your line with a 'P'.

b | During the journey, the position of the Sun in the sky changes.
Draw a line on the diagram that shows the movement of the Sun in the morning.
Label the line 'S'.

Test A

16 Some children have three magnets.

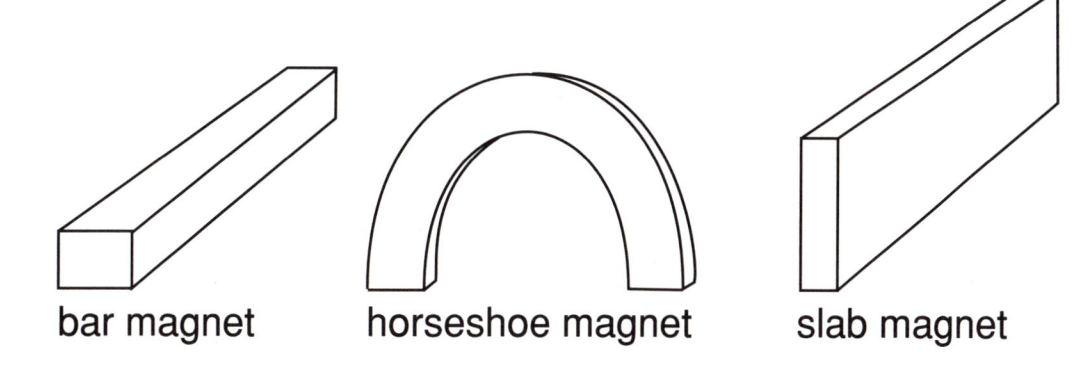

bar magnet   horseshoe magnet   slab magnet

They are trying to find out which is strongest.
They find that each magnet can pick up a drawing pin.

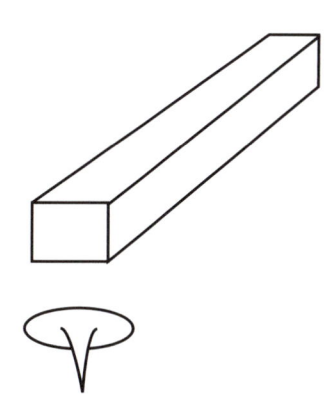

a Draw an arrow to show the pull of the magnet on the drawing pin.

1

Q16a
Level 4

Test A

They find out how many drawing pins each magnet can pick up at a time.
Here are their results.

magnet	number of drawing pins
bar	28
horseshoe	23
slab	35

b Finish the bar chart. Draw a bar to show how many drawing pins each magnet picked up.

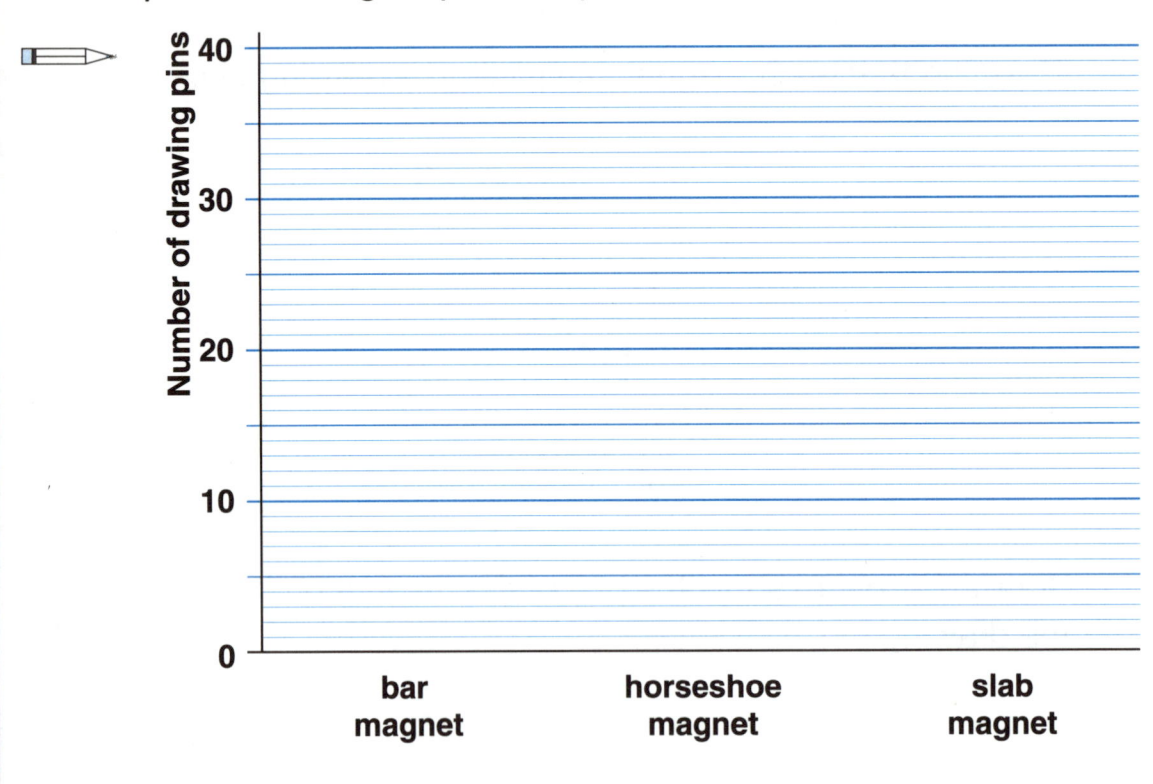

c Which magnet is strongest?

....

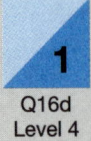

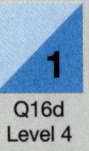

d Explain how you can tell.

....

Test A

17 Benji is making a model of the Earth, Sun and Moon.
He uses a lamp for the Sun and a football for the Earth.

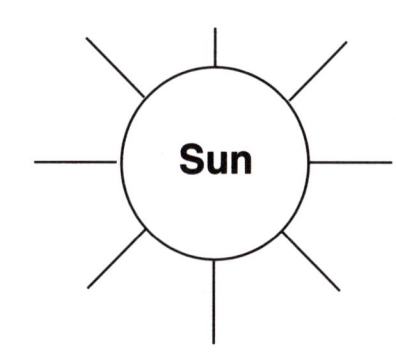

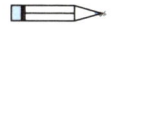

Sun   Earth

a Shade the part of the Earth that is in darkness.

b Benji wants to show his friend how day becomes night.

What should Benji do to show this?
Write or draw on the diagram.

....

c i What could Benji use for the Moon?

....

ii Draw it in the correct place on the diagram.

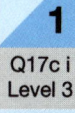

18 Petra makes this circuit.

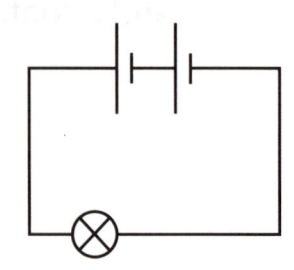

The bulb lights to its normal brightness.

Describe the bulbs in each of the next circuits.
Use words from the list.

bright   dim   normal   off

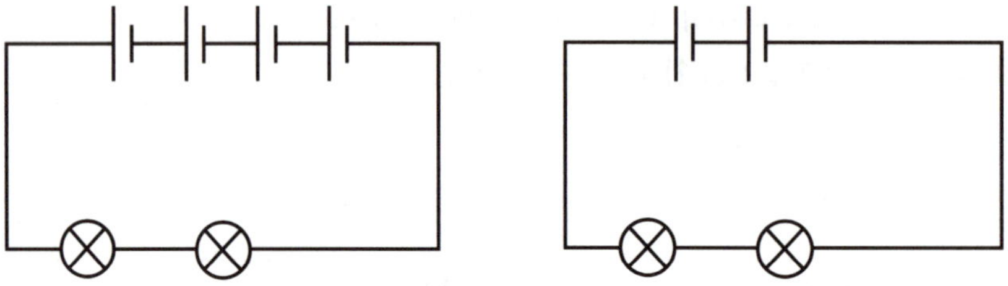

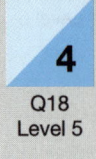

A ....   B ....

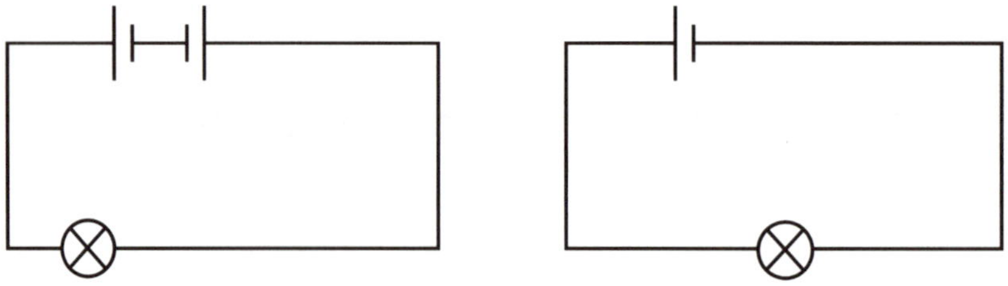

C ....   D ....

19   Daniel is holding a balloon.
     The balloon is filled with helium.

     Upward push from the air

     Downward pull of the Earth

     Explain what happens to the balloon when Daniel lets go.

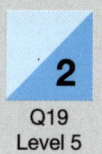

     ....

     ....

     ....

     ....

TEST B
LEVELS 3–5

MARKS

Test B

Start ☐ Finish ☐

1 The drawing shows plants and animals around a pond.

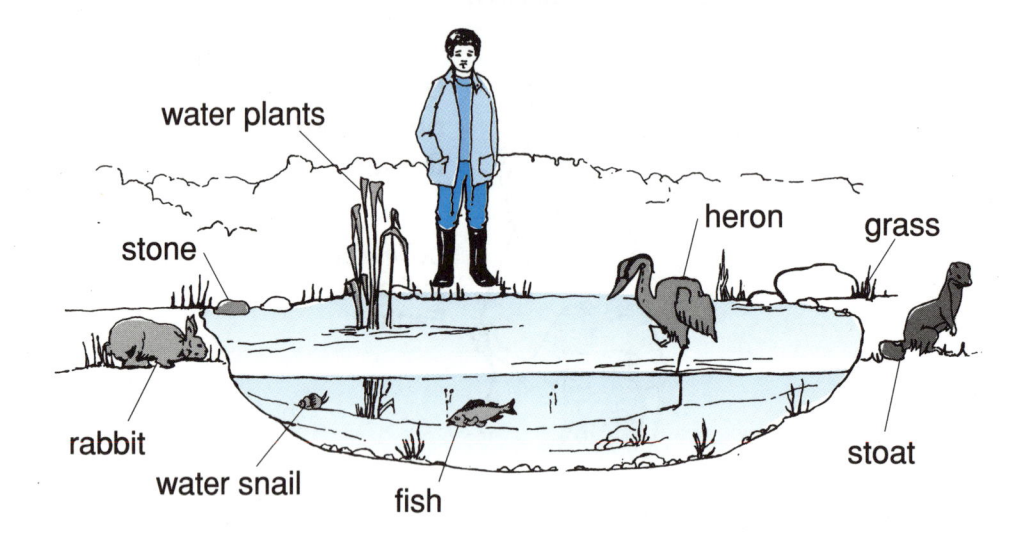

Labels on drawing: water plants, stone, rabbit, water snail, fish, heron, grass, stoat

a Finish the table by writing the name of each thing in the correct column.

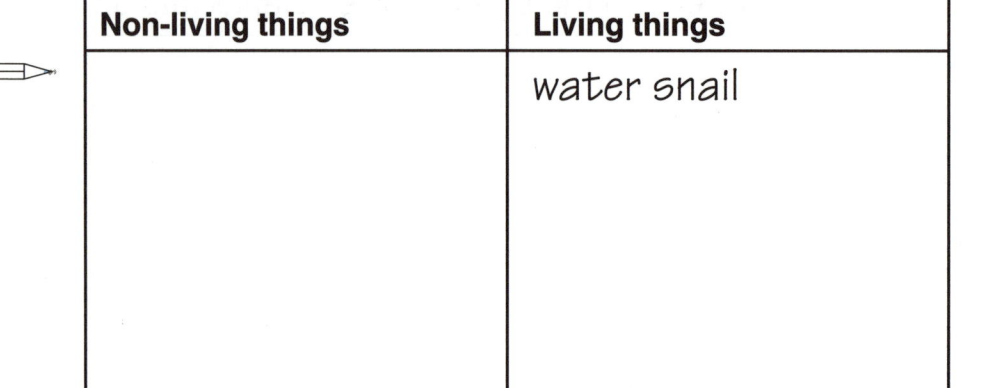

Non-living things	Living things
	water snail

3
Q1a
Level 3

b Write down **two** things that living things can do but non-living things cannot do.

1 ....

2 ....

2
Q1b
Level 3

22

c Snails eat water plants.
Fish eat snails.

Finish these two food chains using the things in the drawing.

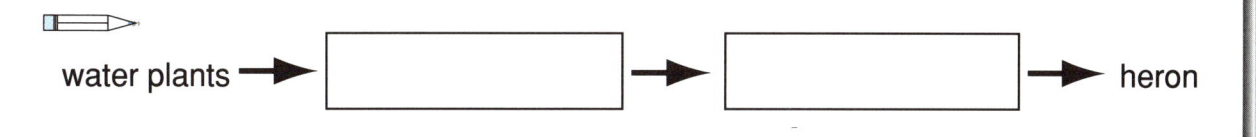

water plants ➡ ☐ ➡ ☐ ➡ heron

☐ ➡ rabbit ➡ ☐

d Write down the names of **two** producers shown in the drawing.

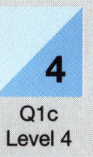

1 ....

2 ....

TEST B
LEVELS 3–5

MARKS

2   The diagram shows the different teeth in your mouth.

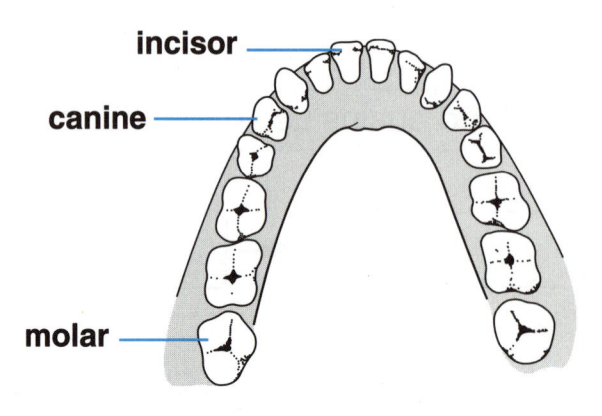

   incisor
   canine
   molar

1
Q2a i
Level 3

a   i   Which teeth rip or tear food?

   ✏ ....

1
Q2a ii
Level 3

   ii   Which teeth grind food into small pieces?

   ✏ ....

1
Q2a iii
Level 3

   iii   Which teeth cut food?

   ✏ ....

b   What **two** things can you do to keep your teeth healthy?
   Tick **two** boxes.

   ✏   brush your teeth after meals   ☐

       drink lots of water   ☐

       eat lots of sweets   ☐

2
Q2b
Level 3

       visit the dentist regularly   ☐

24

3   The diagram shows some organs in the body.

a   Use words from the list to label the organs.

brain   heart   kidney   lung   stomach

B ....
C ....
D ....
A ....
E ....

b   Write down in the table the name of each organ next to the job it does.

job that the organ does	organ
digests food	
filters the blood	
exchanges gases	
controls the body	
pumps blood	

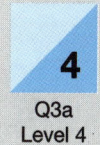

4   The diagram shows the stages in the life cycle of a flowering plant.

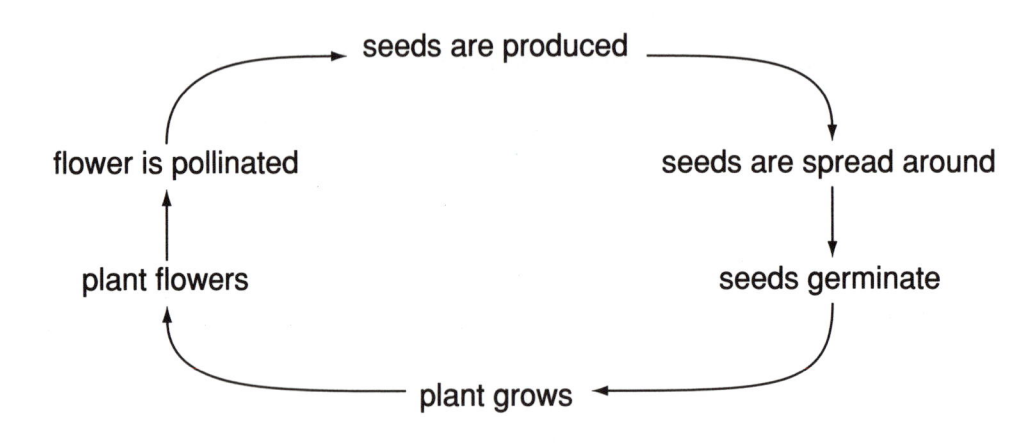

```
          → seeds are produced ─┐
         │                       ↓
flower is pollinated      seeds are spread around
         ↑                       │
         │                       ↓
   plant flowers           seeds germinate
         ↑                       │
         └──── plant grows ←─────┘
```

a   Which stage is often done by insects?

    ....

b   What happens during germination?

    ....

c   Write down **two** conditions needed for seeds to germinate.

    1 ....

    2 ....

d   At which stage is pollen transferred to the stigma?

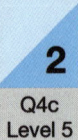

    ....

Test B

5   People have made bricks from clay for many thousands of years.

a   Here are the steps:

   A   Leave to dry in sunlight.
   B   Shape the clay in a mould.
   C   Heat in an oven.
   D   Allow to cool.
   E   Dig out the clay from the ground.

   Put these statements in the correct order.
   One has been done for you.

   | | | A | | |

b   Is the change from clay to brick reversible or not reversible? Explain your answer.

   ....

c   Houses can be made of bricks or stone.

Tick **two** reasons why bricks are better than stone for making houses.

bricks are easier to paint ☐

bricks are lighter ☐

bricks have regular shapes ☐

bricks are waterproof ☐

d   Here are some more materials which can be used for building a house. One of these materials is **natural** and the others have been made.

Tick one box for each material to show if it is made or natural.

material	natural	made
glass		
wood		
plastic		

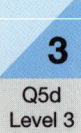

6 The picture shows four methods of transport.

These methods of transport use different fuels. Some fuels are solid, some are liquid and some are gases.

a Finish the table by adding the word solid, liquid or gas.
   One has been done for you.

method of transport	fuel used	fuel is solid, liquid or gas
steam train	coal	
car	petrol	
hot-air balloon	propane	gas
aeroplane	paraffin	

b A steam train and a car are made mainly of iron.
   A hot-air balloon is made mainly of plastics.

   Why is iron not used to make a hot-air balloon?

   ....

7 Chris and Anna are looking at some rocks and comparing some of the properties of the rocks.
The table shows their results.

rock	crystalline or not crystalline	size of crystals or grains	hard or soft	increase in weight when soaked in water
A	Yes – two types of crystals – black ones and white ones	medium	hard	5%
B	No	small	soft	100%
C	No	large	hard	35%

a How does this information show that **A** is a mixture rather than a pure substance?

....

b Which rock absorbs water best?

....

c Why is rock **B** not suitable for re-surfacing roads?

....

d Soils in some parts of the country are **clay** soils and others are **sandy** soils.

Which type of soil feels smooth?

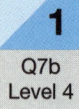

....

e   Some children test a clay soil and a sandy soil.

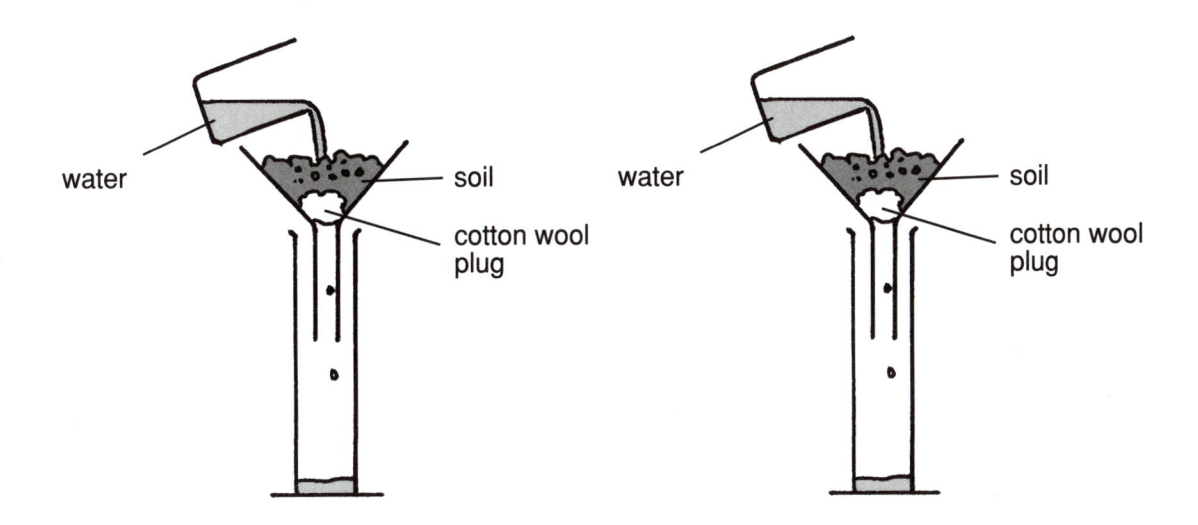

They put equal amounts in two funnels with cottonwool plugs. They then pour equal volumes of water on the soils and measure how long it takes for the water to be collected.

> Explain why water passes through the sandy soil faster than through the clay soil.

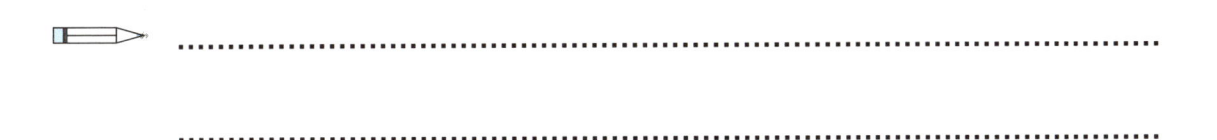

....

....

2

Q7e
Level 4

8   Some children are testing different things to see which dissolve in water.
    Here are some of the things they test.

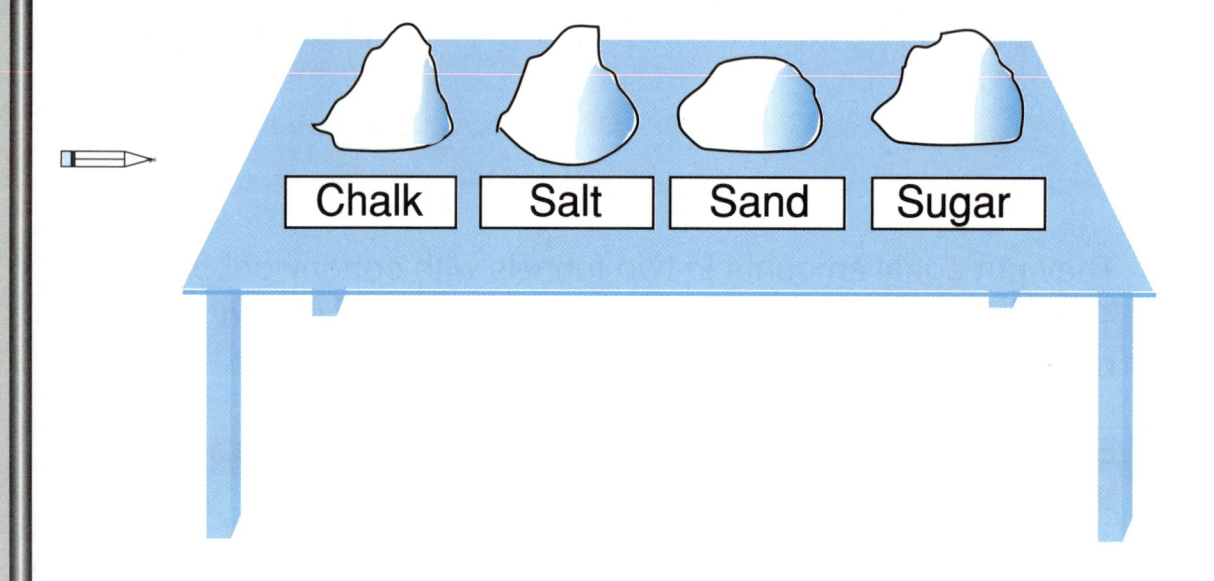

    Chalk   Salt   Sand   Sugar

a   Put a ring round the **two** materials that dissolve in water.

b   How can they tell whether a material has dissolved in the water?

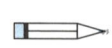

    ....

Test B

They then add some blue crystals to some cold water in a beaker.

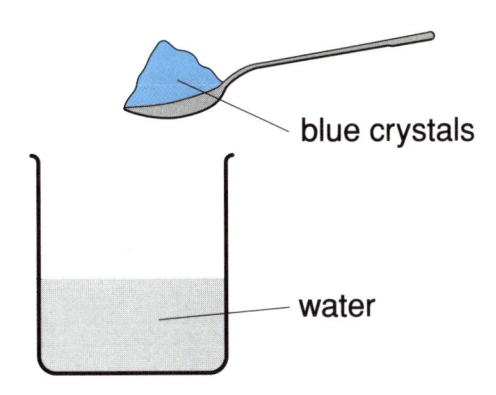

— blue crystals

— water

c Why does the water turn blue?

....

d After stirring the crystals and the water, some crystals are left at the bottom.

Why are some crystals left at the bottom?

....

e How can they separate the crystals from the liquid?

....

f Explain how they can recover the blue crystals from the blue liquid.

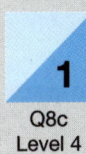

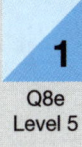

....

....

....

9   Rosie parks her car outside her house.
    When she gets into her car on a cold morning she cannot see out of the windows because they are misted up.

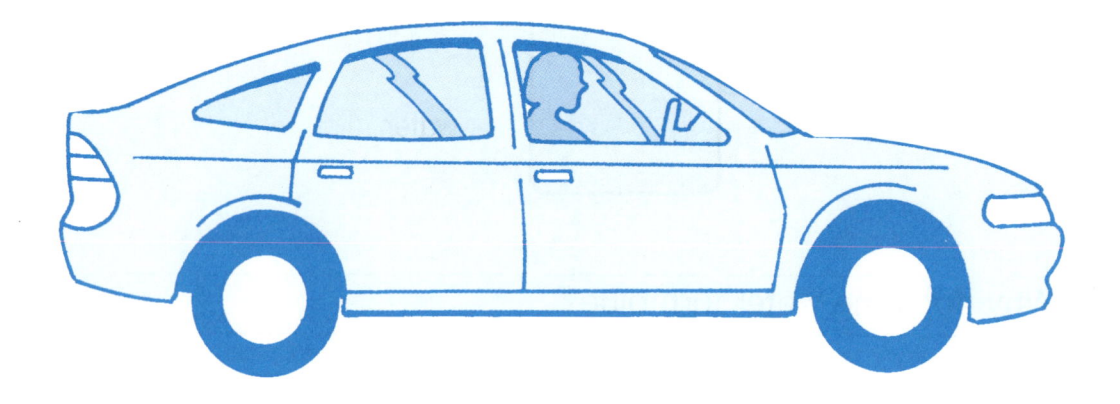

a   How do Rosie's car windows become misted up?

    ....

    ....

    ....

b   When Rosie switches on the air blower, the windows clear.

    How does blowing air on the windows make them clear?

    ....

    ....

10   Emma and Susan make this circuit to test which materials conduct electricity.

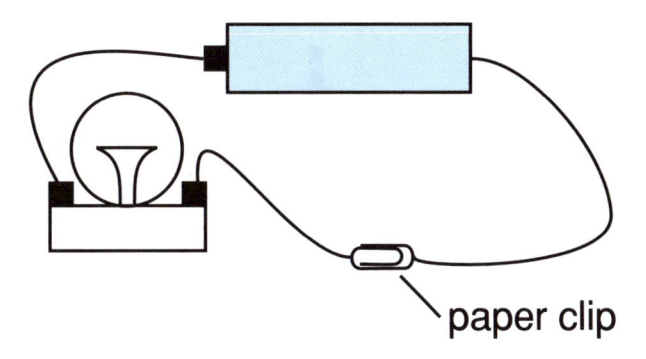

The bulb lights when a metal paper clip is placed in the gap.

Which other materials will cause the bulb to light?
Put a tick or cross by each object in the table.

object	bulb lights (✓ or ✗)
metal paper clip	✓
plastic ruler	
brass screw	
wood block	

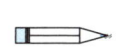

11   A snooker ball bounces off a cushion.

a   **Which diagram shows the force on the ball?**

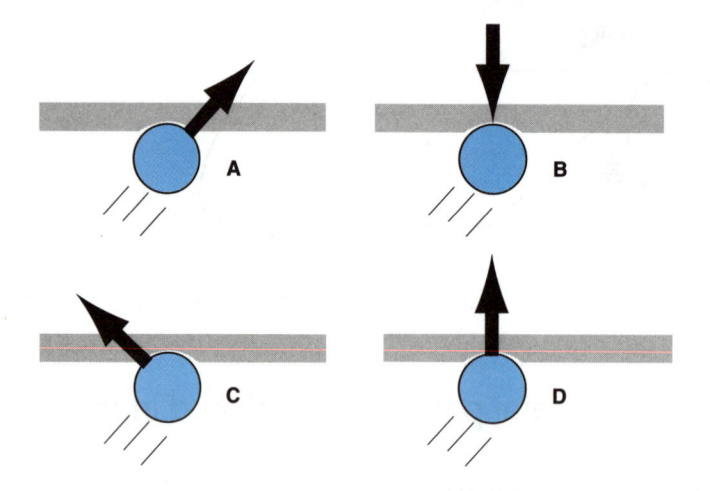

A ☐   B ☐   C ☐   D ☐

b   **Tick two boxes that show two things that change when the ball bounces off the cushion.**

the colour of the ball ☐

the direction of the ball ☐

the shape of the cushion ☐

the colour of the cushion ☐

12 Sam, Tara and Ahmed can all hear the sound from an ice cream van.

a | Who hears the loudest sound?

....

b | Explain why this person hears the loudest sound.

....

13 A child sits on a bouncy toy.

a **i** What happens to the spring when the child sits on the toy?

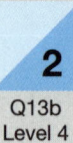

....

ii Why does this happen?

....

b Complete the sentences to describe the two forces acting on the child.
Use words from this list.

        Earth   **pull**   **push**   **spring**

The downward force is the .... of the ....

The upward force is the .... of the ....

c   The arrows on the diagrams show the sizes of the upward and downward forces on the child.

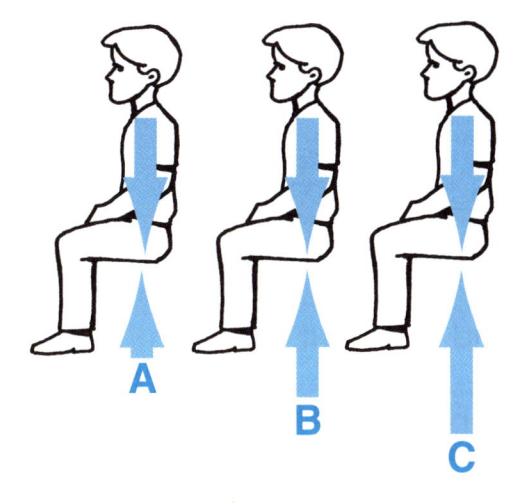

i   Which diagram shows the forces when the child is sitting still?

▢

ii Which diagram shows the forces when his brother pushes him down and lets go?

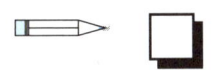

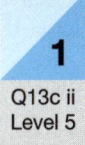

▢

14 Jill and Adam have made a circuit that lights three bulbs.

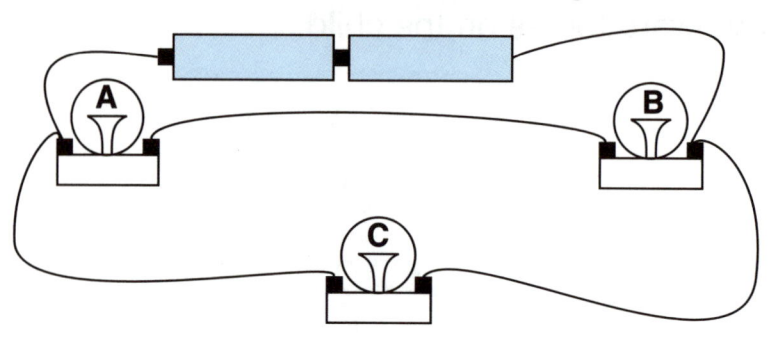

Bulb A 'blows' and goes out.

a What happens to bulb B?

    ....

b What happens to bulb C?

    ....

They then add three switches to their circuit.

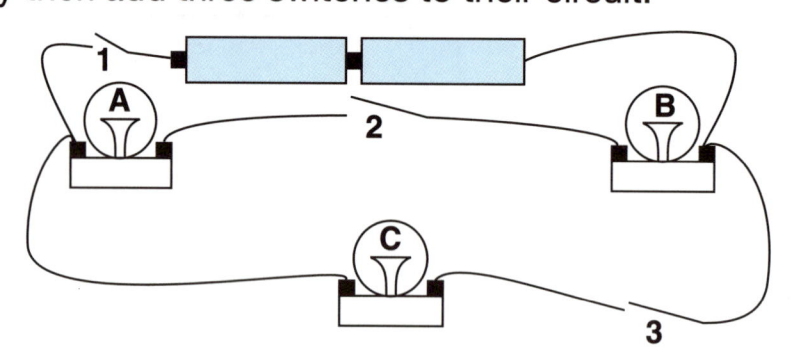

c Switch 1 is turned on. How many bulbs light?

    ....

d Use ticks and crosses in the table on page 41 to show which bulbs are operated by switches 2 and 3.

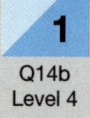

switch	bulbs operated		
	A	B	C
2			
3			

e All the bulbs are now switched on.

Which bulb has the most current passing through it?

....

15 Sammy looks at her face in a mirror.

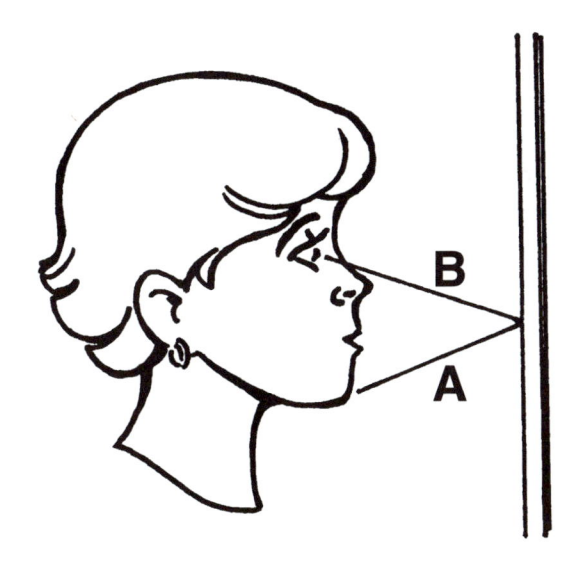

a Draw one arrowhead on each of lines A and B to show how the light travels.

b Which word describes what happens to the light at the mirror? Circle your choice.

deflection   inflection   reflection   refraction

41

16 Tommy uses a torch and a cardboard shape to make a shadow picture on a wall.

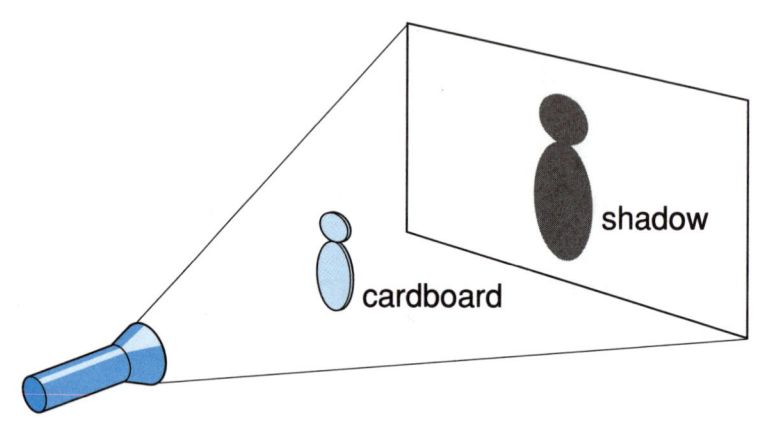

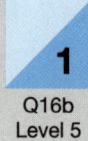

a Explain how the shadow is formed.

   ....

b How does the size of the shadow change when the cardboard is moved towards the torch?

   ....

Test B

17 On a summer morning, Peter sits out in the garden.

a How does Peter stay cool?

....

1 — Q17a Level 3

b By mid-day, the shadow of the tree has changed.

Write down **two** ways in which the shadow changes.

....

....

2 — Q17b Level 5

c Explain how the position of the Sun causes these changes. Give **two** reasons.

....

....

2 — Q17c Level 5

Level 6

1 The diagram illustrates the process of photosynthesis.

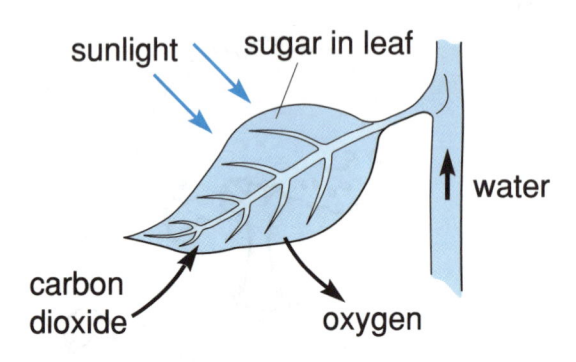

[Diagram of a leaf showing: sunlight and sugar in leaf at top, water entering from the stem, carbon dioxide entering and oxygen leaving at the bottom.]

a What is the source of energy for photosynthesis?

....

b What two substances are used by a plant to make food?

....

....

c Explain why most photosynthesis takes place near the upper surface of a leaf.

....

....

d The diagram shows the exchange of gases when photosynthesis is taking place.

Explain why this gas exchange is reversed at night.

....

....

Level 6

2 Some magnesium ribbon is weighed in a dish. The mass of the ribbon and the dish is 35.46 g. The magnesium is then burned.

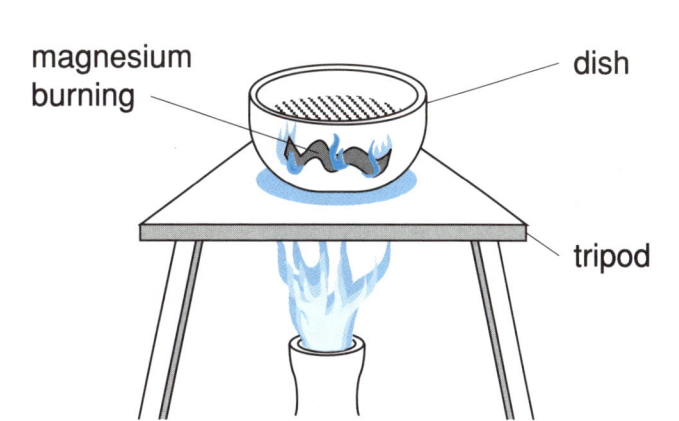

a Which gas does the magnesium react with when it burns? Put a ring round your choice.

carbon dioxide   **hydrogen**   **nitrogen**   **oxygen**

b Finish the word equation for the reaction.

magnesium + ... → ....

c After the magnesium has burned and the dish has cooled, the dish and contents are weighed.
The mass of the ash and the dish is 35.89 g.

Explain why the ash weighs more than the magnesium.

....

....

d How could you show that magnesium is a metal but the ash is a non-metal?

....

....

LEVEL 6

3 The arrows show the horizontal forces acting on a car that is travelling along a level road.

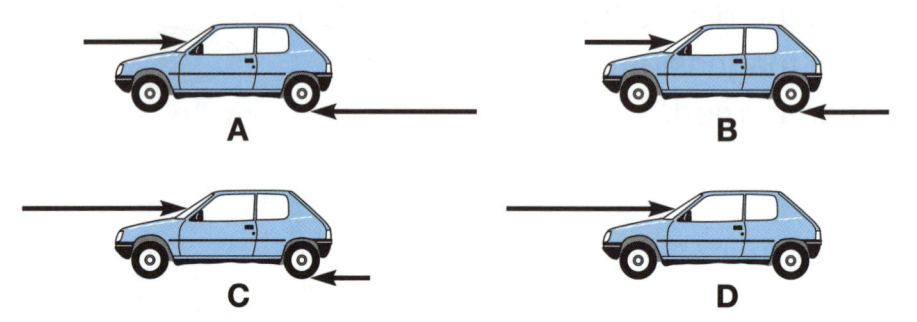

A

B

C

D

a How can you tell that car B is travelling at a steady speed?

....

b How can you tell that car D is braking?

....

c How does the movement of car A differ from that of car C?

....

....

d Put a ring round the arrow that shows the driving force acting on car A.

Level 6

4 a Choose words to finish the sentence about breathing.

air   carbon dioxide

nitrogen   oxygen

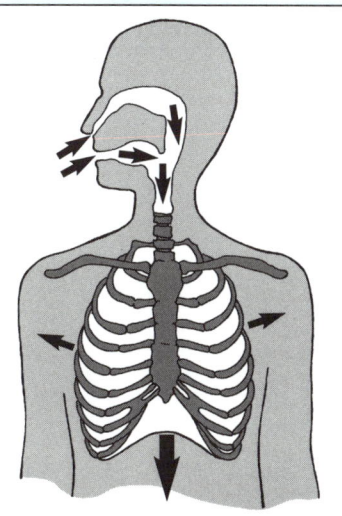

When we breathe in, ……………………

is taken into the lungs. The lungs

absorb …………………… and give

out waste …………………… .

b How do the diaphragm and rib cage move when we breathe in?

Diaphragm: ……………………………………………………………………………

Ribcage: ……………………………………………………………………………

5 Copper oxide is formed when copper is heated in air.

a Underline the type of reaction taking place when copper is heated.

combustion   oxidation

reduction   thermal decomposition

b Write a word equation for the reaction taking place.

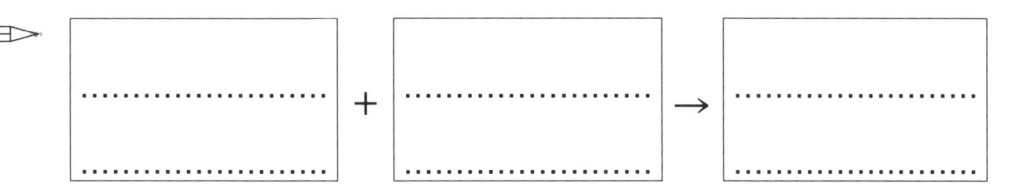

…………………… + …………………… → ……………………

6 The drawing shows the positions of the three planets that are closest to the Sun.

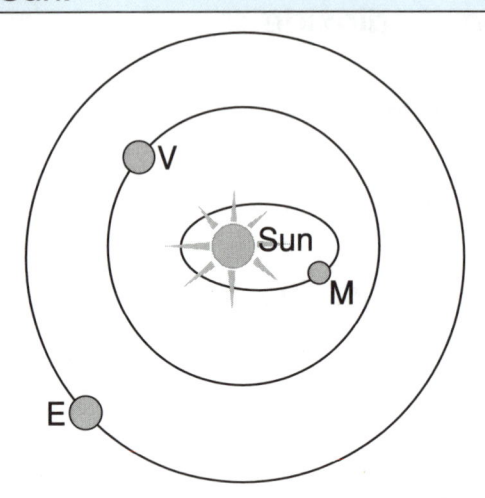

a The times taken by the planets to orbit the Sun are shown in the table.

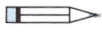

Orbit time	Planet
88 Earth days	
365 Earth days	
225 Earth days	

Write the letter of the correct planet next to its orbit time.

b Explain how a person on planet E is able to see planet M.

....

....

....

Answers

HOW TO MARK THE QUESTIONS

When marking your child's test remember that the answers given are sample answers. You must look at your child's answers and judge whether they deserve credit. Award the mark if the answer deserves credit.

You should pay special attention to spelling. Look at any misspelt word as written and read it aloud. If it sounds correct and has the correct number of syllables, the mark can be awarded. For example, 'desolv' and 'wait' are acceptable as alternatives to 'dissolve' and 'weight'. However, 'photosis' is not correct as an alternative to photosynthesis.

Encourage the correct spelling of scientific words. Look through this book and make a list of scientific words correctly spelt. Reviewing this list in the days before the tests is good preparation for your child.

It is sometimes difficult to know what children mean by their answers. Often, a vague use of the word 'it' can cause confusion. For example, if asked to explain how the experiment showed that Duvet C was warmest, a child may write 'it did not get very cold'. This answer does not make clear whether 'it' refers to Duvet C or the hot-water bottle which retained its heat longest when kept under Duvet C. An ambiguous answer must be marked wrong. When discussing these answers, encourage your child to be very clear about what he or she means, and to replace the word 'it' with the subject in full.

Above all, as you go through the test with your child, try to be positive. Look for good things that have been done in addition to resolving errors.

Enter your child's marks for each test on the Marking Grid on page 62, and then work out his or her level of achievement on these tests on page 61.

Quick Questions — Pages vii, ix, xi

Life processes and living things
1 reproduction
2 incisors
3 arteries
4 skeleton
5 root
6 stem
7 green plant
8 kidney
9 glucose (sugar) and oxygen
10 leaf

Materials and their properties
There may be alternative answers to Q1–5 but any correct answer should be based on properties.
1 Wood is not shiny *or* wood is not heavy *or* wood does not conduct electricity *or* wood does not conduct heat *or* wood breaks when it is bent.
2 Ice cannot be poured *or* ice has a fixed shape *or* ice is a solid.
3 Wood floats *or* steel is magnetic *or* steel is a metal.
4 Sand does not dissolve in water.
5 Water does not burn.
6 melt
7 condense
8 burn
9 melt
10 reversible: 6, 7 and 9; not reversible: 8.

Test A Answers

Physical processes

1. —|⊢—

2. —⊗—

3. ___/

4. pull
5. push
6. by vibrating
7. by vibrating further/bigger vibrations
8. one year
9. one day
10. 28 days

Test A	Pages 1–21

1 a reproduce — 1 mark
grow — 1 mark
b move — 1 mark

Note to parent
There are some characteristics of living things that are also characteristics of non-living things. The swing can move but it cannot reproduce.

c It is too dark. — 1 mark
It is too dry. — 1 mark

Total 5 marks

2 a To catch fish. — 1 mark
b Its tail. — 1 mark
c It keeps them warm. — 1 mark

Note to parent
This question is testing whether your child can recognise simple ways in which an animal is adapted to its environment. In a, do not award a mark for 'to move' or 'because it lives in the water'.

Total 3 marks

3 a B — 1 mark
b C — 1 mark

Note to parent
Your child should appreciate that plants are sensitive to light and grow towards it.

Total 2 marks

4 a It has wings. — 1 mark
It has a long, thin abdomen. — 1 mark
b It does not have wings. — 1 mark
It has more than eight legs. — 1 mark

50

Test A Answers

   c   A spider. *1 mark*

> **Note to parent**
>
> In Key Stage 2 (KS2) your child is not expected to be able to construct a key but is expected to be able to use one. In this question your child is asked to extract information from the given key. You could show your child pictures of the four animals and ask him or her to use the key to identify them.

   d   Put some woodlice in a container where they can choose between a dark area or a light area. *1 mark*
        After leaving them for a while, count the number of woodlice in each area. *1 mark*
   e   Damp *or* moisture *or* water. *1 mark*

> **Note to parent**
>
> This question links with the type of practical activity that your child is likely to carry out in school and can do at home. If your child carries this out at home he or she should return the woodlice to where they were originally found after the investigation.

Total 8 marks

5 a   A: sepal
       B: stamen
       C: stigma
       D: petal
       E: ovary *4 marks*

> **Note to parent**
>
> Award four marks for all five correct in *a* and *b*, three marks for three correct, two marks for two correct and one mark if only one job has been identified correctly.

   b   The completed table is:

Job/part of flower	Letter of part
attracts insects to the plant	D
male part of the flower	B
where egg cells are made	E
sticky part that receives pollen grains	C
protects the flower when in bud	A

4 marks
Total 8 marks

6 a   80 beats per minute. *1 mark*
   b   Sam's pulse rate goes up. *1 mark*
   c   To pump more blood round her body. *1 mark*
   d   After 11 minutes. *1 mark*

Test A Answers

Note to parent

You could show your child how to measure her or his pulse rate using the pulse in the wrist or the neck. He or she could then investigate the effects that exercise and rest have on the pulse rate.
As well as testing whether your child understands how these factors affect pulse rate, this question tests skills in reading data from a graph.

Total 4 marks

7 a Here is the correctly completed table.

material	easy to bend	attracted to a a magnet	see-through	soaks up water
paper	✓	✗	✗	✓
polythene	✓	✗	✓	✗
wood	✗	✗	✗	✗
limestone	✗	✗	✗	✗
aluminium foil	✓	✗	✗	✗
candlewax	✓	✗	✗	✗
iron	✗	✓	✗	✗

Award one mark for each line completed correctly.   5 marks
b Polythene is see-through.   1 mark
Paper soaks up water.   1 mark
c aluminium foil (1 mark) and iron (1 mark)   2 marks

Note to parent

In *c* there is one mark for each correct answer. Do not deduct a mark for a wrong answer.

Total 9 marks

8 a i A   1 mark
  ii C   1 mark
  iii B   1 mark
b filtering *or* filtration   1 mark
c i evaporation   1 mark
  ii Reversible; the granules dissolve in water to make coffee solution.   1 mark

Note to parent

In KS2, children are often confused about the difference between sieving and filtration. *Sieving* uses a large mesh and can be used to separate large solid particles from smaller solid particles. It can also be used to separate large solid particles from a liquid.
Filtering uses a much smaller mesh and so is used to separate small solid particles, such as powders, from a liquid.
Also note that your child has to give the reason to gain a mark in *c ii*.

Total 6 marks

9 a A thermometer.   1 mark
b One container has a lid, the other has no lid.   1 mark
There are different amounts of water in the containers.   1 mark
The containers are made of different materials.   1 mark
c 83°C   1 mark

Test A Answers

d

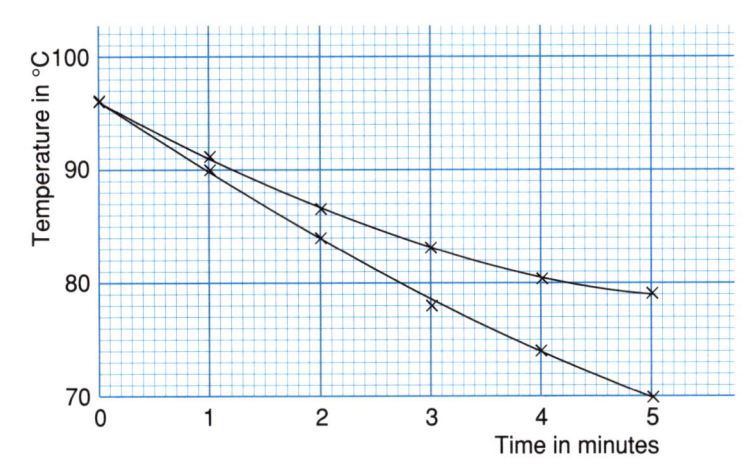

[Graph showing Temperature in °C (y-axis, 70-100) vs Time in minutes (x-axis, 0-5), with two curves plotted]

Two marks for correct plotting (Deduct 1 mark for one mistake).	*2 marks*
Attempt at drawing a curve.	*1 mark*

e The graph for the beaker wrapped in foam goes down faster or further than the one for the beaker wrapped in fur. *1 mark*

Note to parent

Many pupils at the end of KS2 have an understanding of what is meant by a fair test. Everything must be kept the same except for the one thing being varied – in this case the layer of foam or fur. By the end of KS2 it is expected that children are starting to recognise when it is appropriate to use a straight line for a graph and when a curve is more appropriate. Encourage your child to draw a 'best-fit' line or curve rather than just join the points together.

Total 9 marks

10 The completed table is:

water condenses to form clouds	3
water runs into the sea	5
water falls as rain	4
water evaporates from the sea	1
water vapour rises in the air	2

3 marks

Award three marks for all four responses being correct, two marks for two correct responses and one mark for just one correct.

Note to parent

The important processes in the water cycle are evaporation and condensation. You can encourage your child to explain the water cycle to you using these terms correctly.

Total 3 marks

11 a It goes down. *1 mark*
 b Water vapour from the air *1 mark*
 condenses on the glass. *1 mark*

Test A Answers

> **Note to parent**
>
> In KS2 children often find it difficult to appreciate that when water evaporates it changes to water vapour in the air. This water vapour condenses back into water on cold surfaces.

Total 3 marks

12 a The direction of the ball. — *1 mark*
The shape of the ball. — *1 mark*
b The height of the ball. — *1 mark*
The speed of the ball. — *1 mark*

> **Note to parent**
>
> Forces on objects cause a change in shape. This is sometimes noticeable, for example the change in shape of a sagging bookshelf, and sometimes not noticeable, for example the change in shape of a concrete floor when you walk across it. They can also cause a change in the speed and/or direction of a moving object.

Total 4 marks

13 a The circuit is not complete. — *1 mark*
b Add another wire.

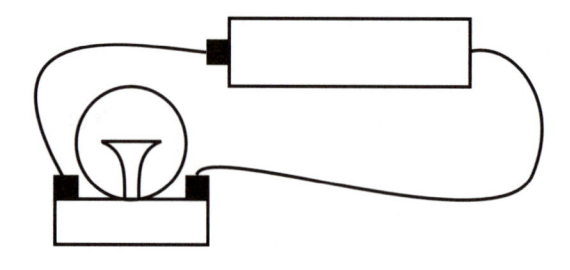

1 mark

> **Note to parent**
>
> One of the first things that children learn about electricity in KS2 is that a complete circuit is needed for a device such as a lamp to work. Your child can practise making circuits at home using a few cheap and readily available components such as some batteries, lamps, a motor and pieces of connecting wire. No special kit is needed.

Total 2 marks

14 a Sarong — *1 mark*
b She is closest to the starter. — *1 mark*
c Mary — *1 mark*
She hears the sound last. — *1 mark*

> **Note to parent**
>
> Children can be made aware that sound takes a finite time to travel by drawing their attention to events where they see something happening before they hear it. A low-flying aircraft is one example of such an event.

Total 4 marks

54

Test A Answers

15 a The line should be reflected at the puddle. *1 mark*
It should bounce off the puddle at the same angle as it hits. *1 mark*

Note to parent
Your child should appreciate that most objects are seen by the light that they reflect. Mirrors and other shiny surfaces reflect light in a regular and predictable way. Other objects are said to *scatter* the light; they reflect it in all directions.

b The line should show the Sun moving higher in the sky. *1 mark*
It should move to the right, following a curved path. *1 mark*
Total 4 marks

16 a The arrow should point vertically upwards. *1 mark*
b Here is the finished bar chart.

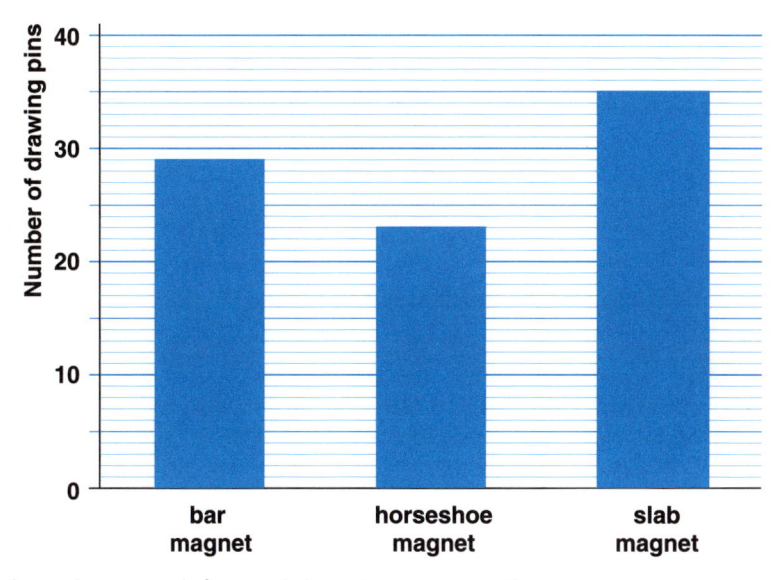

3 marks

Award one mark for each bar drawn correctly.
c The slab magnet. *1 mark*
d It picks up the most drawing pins. *1 mark*

Note to parent
Presenting information as charts and graphs is an important scientific skill that also applies to other areas of study. It will be emphasised throughout your child's secondary school science education.

Total 6 marks

17 a

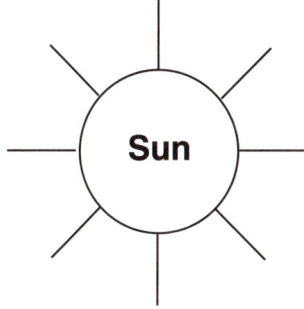

1 mark
b He should turn the Earth round on its own axis. *1 mark*

Test A Answers

> **Note to parent**
>
> Your child may not use this form of words, but make sure that he or she is clear about the different movements of the Earth. One *rotation* on its axis takes one day and causes day and night.
> One *orbit* round the Sun takes one year.

    c i Award a mark for any object that is spherical and smaller than the Earth,
        for example a tennis ball or table tennis ball. *1 mark*
    ii It should be drawn much closer to the Earth than to the Sun. *1 mark*

Total 4 marks

18   A: normal   *1 mark*
       B: dim   *1 mark*
       C: off   *1 mark*
       D: dim   *1 mark*

> **Note to parent**
>
> The bulb in *C* is off because the cells are connected back-to-back, so there is no voltage and no current.

Total 4 marks

19   The balloon rises.   *1 mark*
       Because the upward force is bigger then the downward force.   *1 mark*

> **Note to parent**
>
> Your child should be able to recognise simple situations where forces are balanced and cause no change in movement, and where forces are unbalanced and cause an object to speed up or slow down.

Total 2 marks

Test B Answers

Test B — Pages 22–43

1 a Non-living: stone. *1 mark*
Living: water plants, person, heron, grass, stoat, fish, water snail, rabbit. *2 marks*
Allow 1 mark if one living thing is omitted or placed in the wrong column.

b *Any two from:* feed, sense, respire (*allow* breathe), grow, get rid of waste, reproduce and move. *2 marks*

Note to parent
Do not worry if your child does not know all the characteristics of living things. At KS2 the ones required are feed, move (animals only), grow and reproduce.

c snail (1 mark) fish (1 mark) *2 marks*
grass (1 mark) stoat (1 mark) *2 marks*
d grass *1 mark*
water plants *1 mark*

Note to parent
Your child should be aware that green plants are the producers in a food chain. They are called producers because they make their own food. All the other organisms in the food chain rely on this food.

Total 11 marks

2 a i canines *1 mark*
ii molars *1 mark*
iii incisors *1 mark*
b Brush your teeth after meals. *1 mark*
Visit the dentist regularly. *1 mark*
Total 5 marks

3 a A: kidney
B: brain
C: heart
D: lung
E: stomach *4 marks*
Award four marks for all five correct, three marks for three correct, two marks for two correct and one mark for one correct.

b Here is the completed table:

job that the organ does	organ
digests food	stomach
filters the blood	kidney
exchanges gases	lung
controls the body	brain
pumps blood	heart

5 marks

Award one mark for each correct organ.

Test B Answers

Note to parent
Children working at level 4 should be able to identify the major organs in the body.
At level 5, they should be able to describe the jobs that these organs do.

Total 9 marks

4	a	pollination	1 mark
	b	The seeds sprout.	1 mark
	c	warmth	1 mark
		moisture/damp/water	1 mark
	d	pollination	1 mark

Note to parent
Your child should be able to link the correct scientific names to each of the stages in the life cycle of a flowering plant. Wild flowers or flowers from a garden can be dissected without using special tools to study the different parts of a flower.

Total 5 marks

5 a The correct order is:
E B A C D *2 marks*
Award 2 marks if fully correct, and 1 mark if two are correct.
 b Not reversible. The bricks (or brick dust) do not make clay if mixed with water. *1 mark*

Note to parent
To gain the mark in *b*, your child needs to give a correct reason as well as the correct answer.

 c Bricks are lighter. *1 mark*
    Bricks have regular shapes. *1 mark*

 d Here is the completed table:

material	natural	made
glass		✓
wood	✓	
plastic		✓

3 marks

Award one mark for each correct row.

Note to parent
Your child should be able to classify a range of materials as made or natural. Many natural materials are in short supply or have inferior properties to made materials and are being replaced by materials that are made, i.e. where the natural material has been processed to change its properties.

Total 8 marks

6 a Steam train – coal/solid. *1 mark*
     Car – petrol/liquid. *1 mark*
     Aeroplane – paraffin/liquid. *1 mark*
 b   Iron is too heavy or too dense. *1 mark*

Total 4 marks

Test B Answers

7	**a**	A has two different types of crystal.	*1 mark*
	b	B	*1 mark*
	c	It is soft *or* soaks up too much water.	*1 mark*
	d	clay	*1 mark*

Note to parent

Clay feels smooth because it is made up of small particles. Sandy soil is gritty because the particles are larger.

	e	Sandy soil is made of larger particles.	*1 mark*
		The water can travel more easily through the spaces between the particles.	*1 mark*

Note to parent

Your child should be aware that different types of soil have different rates of drainage.

Total 6 marks

8	**a**	salt	*1 mark*
		sugar	*1 mark*
	b	The water goes clear *or* there is no material left at the bottom.	*1 mark*
	c	The blue crystals have dissolved.	*1 mark*
	d	No more will dissolve.	*1 mark*
	e	By filtering.	*1 mark*
	f	Heat the liquid *or* leave it in a warm place.	*1 mark*
		So that the water evaporates.	*1 mark*

Note to parent

Dissolving substances and making crystals are science tasks that your child can carry out at home with no special equipment. Alum is a suitable substance for your child to use for crystal growing.

Total 8 marks

9	**a**	There is water vapour in the air.	*1 mark*
		This condenses on the windows.	*1 mark*
	b	The water evaporates.	*1 mark*
		The air takes away the water vapour.	*1 mark*

Note to parent

It is worth emphasising to your child that washing dries quicker on a windy day than on a calm day, because the wind removes the water vapour from around the washing.

Total 4 marks

10

object	bulb lights (✓ or ✗)
metal paper clip	✓
plastic ruler	✗
brass screw	✓
wood block	✗

3 marks

Award one mark for each correct row.

Test B Answers

> **Note to parent**
>
> Children are often confused about electricity and magnetism. They frequently think that all metals conduct electricity and all metals are magnetic. One important characteristic of metals is that they do conduct electricity, but of the common metals only iron, nickel and steel are magnetic.

Total 3 marks

11 a B   *1 mark*

> **Note to parent**
>
> Diagram B is the only one that shows a force acting on the ball.

   b The direction of the ball.   *1 mark*
       The shape of the cushion.   *1 mark*

Total 3 marks

12 a Sam   *1 mark*
   b He is closest to the ice cream van.   *1 mark*

Total 2 marks

13 a i It is squashed or gets smaller.   *1 mark*
    ii There is a force pushing down on it.   *1 mark*
   b pull; Earth   *Both words required.*   *1 mark*
       push; spring   *Both words required.*   *1 mark*

> **Note to parent**
>
> It is not only at KS2 that children find forces difficult. The best approach is to teach that forces are caused by objects and act on other objects, so all forces can be described as 'object A pulls/pushes object B'. Use of the term 'gravity' is confusing; it leads children to talk about gravity as if it were an object. The downward force that acts on objects is best described as 'the Earth's pull'.

   c i B   *1 mark*
    ii C   *1 mark*

Total 6 marks

14 a It goes out.   *1 mark*
   b It stays lit or nothing happens.   *1 mark*
   c None   *1 mark*
   d The completed table is:

switch	bulbs operated		
	A	B	C
2	✓	✓	✗
3	✗	✗	✓

2 marks

Award one mark for each correct row.
   d C   *1 mark*

Test B Answers

> **Note to parent**
>
> If your child has difficulty with this, explain that A and B form one circuit, with two batteries to two bulbs and C forms a separate circuit, with two batteries to one bulb.

Total 6 marks

15 a The arrowhead on A should point to the mirror. *1 mark*
   b The arrowhead on B should point to the eye. *1 mark*

> **Note to parent**
>
> Children's confusion about seeing is often due to them thinking that eyes give out light. You can explain to them that light is only given out by light sources such as lamps and television screens. Other objects are seen by the light that they reflect.

   b reflection *1 mark*

Total 3 marks

16 a The light does not pass through the cardboard. *1 mark*
   b It gets bigger. *1 mark*

> **Note to parent**
>
> Children can enjoy learning about shadows by making a shadow puppet theatre. All that is needed is some cardboard, a battery and a torch lamp.

Total 2 marks

17 a By sitting in the shadow. *1 mark*
   b It becomes shorter. *1 mark*
      It changes position. *1 mark*
   c The Sun is higher in the sky. *1 mark*
      The Sun has moved across the sky. *1 mark*

> **Note to parent**
>
> A much better answer to c is that the Sun seems to have moved across the sky or the Earth has rotated on its axis.

Total 5 marks

Level 6 Answers

Level 6 — Pages 44–46

1   **a**   The Sun *or* sunlight. — *1 mark*
    b   Water and carbon dioxide. *One mark each.* — *2 marks*
    c   There is more sunlight on the upper surface than on the lower surface. — *1 mark*
        The chloroplasts are near the upper surface. — *1 mark*
    d   At night the plant respires but does not photosynthesise. — *1 mark*
        Respiration uses oxygen and produces carbon dioxide as a waste product. — *1 mark*

> **Note to parent**
>
> Children working at level 6 should realise that photosynthesis and respiration both occur in plants. However, while the plant is respiring all the time, it only photosynthesises in the light.

Total 7 marks

2   **a**   oxygen — *1 mark*
    b   oxygen (*1 mark*); magnesium oxide (*1 mark*) — *2 marks*

> **Note to parent**
>
> At level 6 children are expected to be able to write simple word equations.

    c   The magnesium has combined with oxygen. — *1 mark*
    d   Test to see if they conduct electricity. — *1 mark*
        Magnesium is a conductor and the ash is not. — *1 mark*

Total 6 marks

3   **a**   The forces are balanced (equal in size and opposite in direction). — *1 mark*
    b   There is no forwards force, only a backwards force. — *1 mark*
    c   A is speeding up. — *1 mark*
        C is slowing down. — *1 mark*
    d   The ring should be around the arrow that points forwards (to the left on the page). *1 mark*

> **Note to parent**
>
> At level 6 children are expected to understand how the motion of an object such as a car depends on the balance of the forces that act on it.

Total 5 marks

4   **a**   Air
        Oxygen
        Carbon dioxide — *3 marks*
    b   Diaphragm moves down. — *1 mark*
        Ribcage moves out. — *1 mark*

> **Note to parent**
>
> It is important to stress to your child the need to study all the information given in the question. The answers to b are shown on the diagram.

Total 5 marks

Level 6 Answers

5 a Oxidation — *1 mark*
  b Copper + oxygen → copper oxide — *2 marks*
  Award one mark for the left-hand side and one mark for the right-hand side of the equation.

Note to parent
At Level 6 your child will be expected to write simple word equations. In this case it is a matter of using the information given.

Total 3 marks

6 a M
  E
  V
  Three correct: 2 marks; two correct: 1 mark — *2 marks*
  b M is hit by light from the Sun. — *1 mark*
  It reflects light in all directions. — *1 mark*

Total 4 marks

Notes

Determining your child's level

FINDING YOUR CHILD'S LEVEL IN TESTS A AND B
When you have marked a test, enter the total number of marks your child scored for each question on the Marking Grid overleaf. Then add them up and enter the test total on the grid.

Using the total for each test, look at the chart below to determine your child's level for each test.

Test A or Test B

Level 2 or below	Level 3	Level 4	Level 5
up to 19	20–32	33–59	60+

FINDING YOUR CHILD'S OVERALL LEVEL IN SCIENCE
After you have worked out separate levels for Tests A and B, add up your child's total marks for the two tests. Use this total and the chart below to determine your child's overall level in Science. The chart also shows you how your child's level in these tests compares with the target level for his or her age group.

Total for Tests A and B

Level 2 or below	Level 3	Level 4	Level 5
up to 38	39–64	65–118	119+
	Working towards target level for age group	Working at target level	Working beyond target level

Level 6 sample questions
If your child achieved Level 5 in Tests A and B, you may want to see how he or she does on the Level 6 sample questions. A score of 20 or higher on the sample Level 6 questions indicates that your child is working beyond the target level, at Level 6.

Marking Grid

TEST A *Pages 1–21*

Question	Marks available	Marks scored	Question	Marks available	Marks scored
1	5		11	3	
2	3		12	4	
3	2		13	2	
4	8		14	4	
5	8		15	4	
6	4		16	6	
7	9		17	4	
8	6		18	4	
9	9		19	2	
10	3				
			Total	90	

TEST B *Pages 22–43*

Question	Marks available	Marks scored	Question	Marks available	Marks scored
1	11		10	3	
2	5		11	3	
3	9		12	2	
4	5		13	6	
5	8		14	6	
6	4		15	3	
7	6		16	2	
8	8		17	5	
9	4				
			Total	90	

LEVEL 6 *Pages 44–48*

Question	Marks available	Marks scored	Question	Marks available	Marks scored
1	7		4	5	
2	6		5	3	
3	5		6	4	
			Total	30	